THE EAST COAST
main line since 1925

THE EAST COAST
main line since 1925

K. Hoole

LONDON

IAN ALLAN LTD

First published 1977

ISBN 0 7110 0780 2

Published by Ian Allan Ltd, Shepperton, Surrey,
and printed in the United Kingdom by
Ian Allan Printing Ltd.

Contents

Introduction	7
1925–1929	9
1930–1934	25
1935–1939	40
1940–1944	61
1945–1949	68
1950–1954	78
1955–1959	86
1960–1964	98
1965–1969	113
1970–1975	120
Appendix 1	125
Appendix 2	126
Appendix 3	126
Appendix 4	127
Appendix 5	127
Appendix 6	128

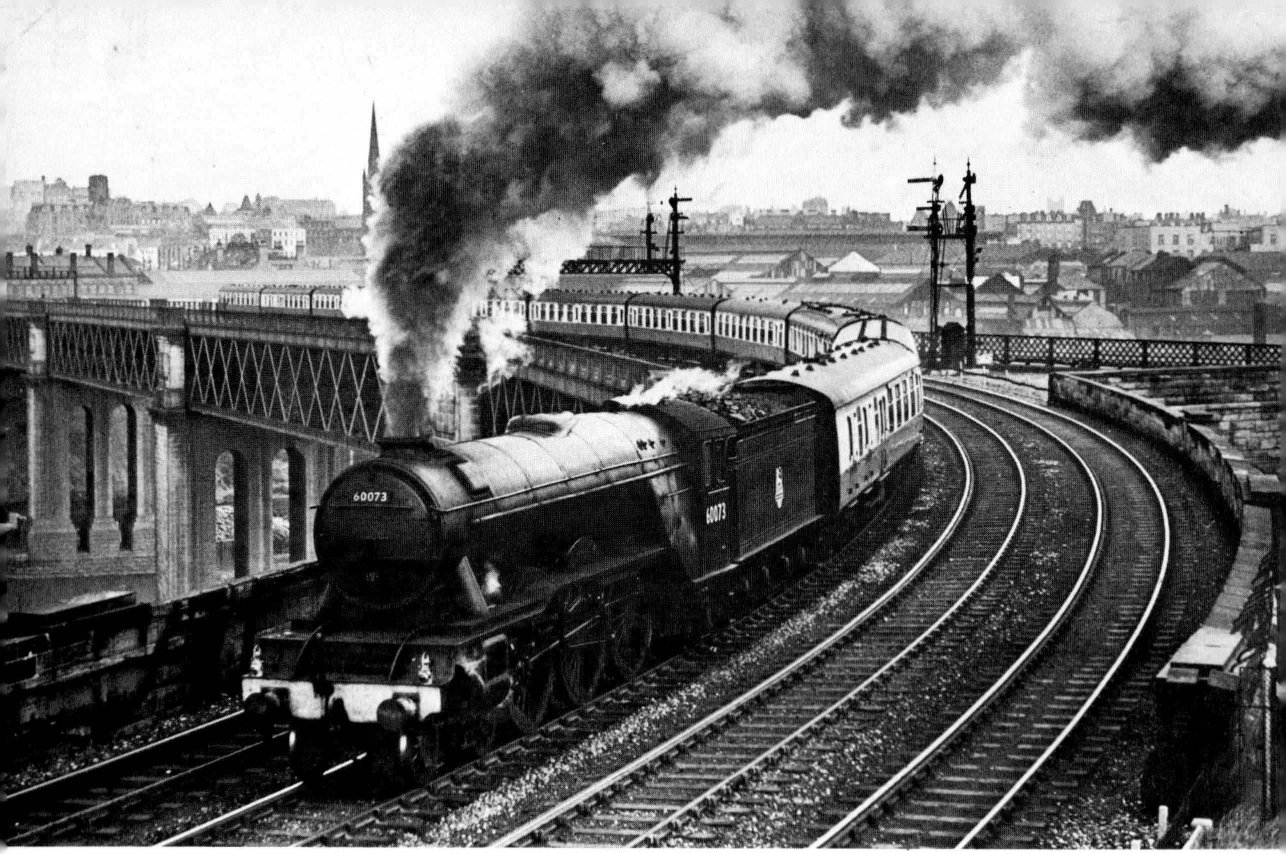
60073
60073

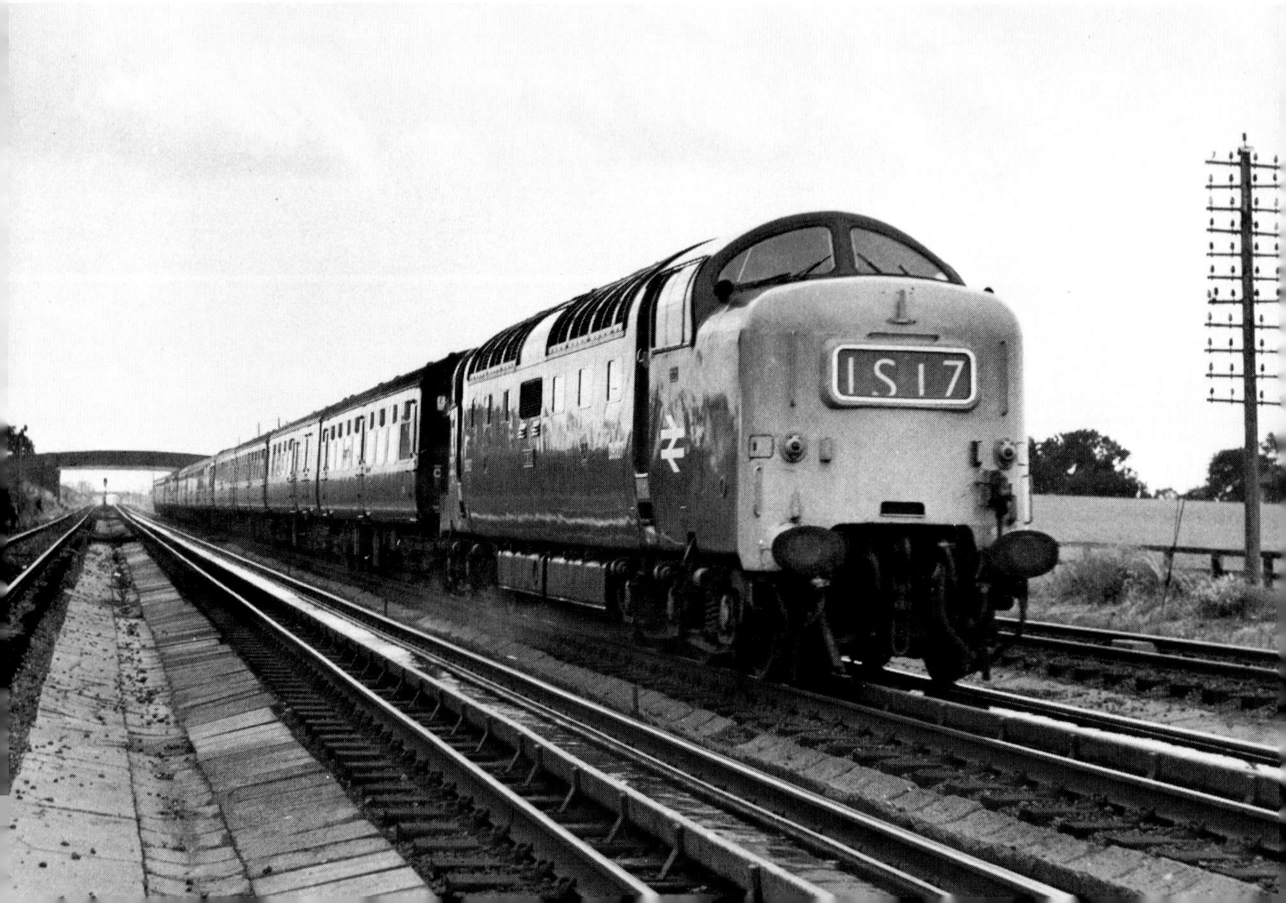
1S17

Introduction

The East Coast main line was an amalgam of three companies, the Great Northern between Kings Cross and Shaftholme Junction, the North Eastern from Shaftholme Junction to Berwick, and the North British from Berwick to Waverley station, Edinburgh. These three companies had worked closely together since the 1860s, united against a common enemy on the West Coast (L&NWR and Caledonian) and from 1860 a jointly-owned stock of vehicles had formed the East Coast Joint Stock fleet, which ceased to exist as such when the three companies concerned became part of the LNER at Grouping on 1 January 1923. However, the vehicles used on main-line services were kept separate from the normal Area stocks and could be distinguished by having the figure 1 as the first digit of their numbers, after a brief period with a J suffix.

Although the main line was formerly owned by three companies the services were worked by the engines of only two – the Great Northern between London and York, and the North Eastern between York and Edinburgh. This was because, under an Agreement of 12 May 1862, the North Eastern exercised their running powers between Berwick and Edinburgh and until 1923 (except in World War I) North British locomotives did not normally work south of Berwick.

Until 1927/8 the locomotives of the three LNER Areas concerned – Southern, North Eastern, and Southern Scottish – kept fairly closely to their own area and it was as unusual to see a former North Eastern engine on an East Coast express south of York, as it was to see a former Great Northern engine north of York. However, with common ownership and gradually extended locomotive workings it became possible to see Edinburgh engines in London and London engines in Edinburgh.

Under Gresley the LNER adopted a scheme of locomotive classification similar to that used on the Great Northern Railway, where a letter indicated the wheel arrangement and one or two figures following the letter indicated the class in that wheel arrangement. Subsequent developments in a wheel arrangement took the higher numbers. Thus the original Gresley Pacifics were A1; the North Eastern Raven Pacifics were A2; the subsequent high-pressure Gresley Pacifics A3; and the streamlined Pacifics A4. When an engine was rebuilt it was transferred from one class to another: for example, the original Gresley Pacifics when rebuilt with 220lb boilers were reclassified A1 to A3, leaving A1 vacant for new engines by a later designer.

The North Eastern had a somewhat similar system but the letters were used in alphabetical order of appearance from 1886. Thus T. W. Worsdell's 2-4-2T of 1886 was Class A, then going right through the alphabet to the Raven Atlantics of 1911, known as Class Z. In some cases a figure was added to denote an improved version of a class: for instance, Class S covered the first 4-6-0 engines which appeared in 1899; Class S1 the large wheel variety of 1900/1; S2 the large boiler version of 1911; and finally S3 the Raven three-cylinder version of 1919.

The North Eastern painted the class on the front buffer beam of every locomotive and this was continued well into LNER days: in fact, the North Eastern classification was painted on the buffer beam until 1932, but some engines which had been overhauled just prior to the system being abandoned kept the NER class until the mid-1930s. From 1932 the LNER class was placed on the buffer beam.

Thus, through being so clearly visible, and being in use so late, the North Eastern classification was well known and was used almost as frequently as the LNER class: in fact, the NER class is still used to this day amongst those interested in the locomotives of the old company. Consequently in this work the North Eastern class is sometimes quoted, even in LNER days. To avoid confusion the most common NER/LNER equivalents are listed:

NER	Wheels	LNER/BR
S	4-6-0	B13
S1	4-6-0	B14
S2	4-6-0	B15
S3	4-6-0	B16
V & V/09	4-4-2	C6

Above left: Class A3 4-6-2 No. 60073 *St. Gatien* leaving Newcastle on the 12.40pm to Bristol on 25 September 1954. The train is curving to the south off the King Edward Bridge. */S. E. Teasdale*

Left: 'Deltic' No. D9007 *Pinza* passing over Wiske Moor water troughs on the down 'Flying Scotsman' on 19 July 1969. */Ian S. Carr*

Z	4-4-2	C7
4CC	4-4-2	C8
R	4-4-0	D20
R1	4-4-0	D21
P2	0-6-0	J26
P3	0-6-0	J27
T & T1	0-8-0	Q5
T2	0-8-0	Q6
T3	0-8-0	Q7

D49, J39 and K3 were LNER standard classes and thus had no North Eastern classification.

In the above table Class 4CC covered two engines, the Smith 4-Cylinder compounds – hence their classification; and V/09 referred to the modified Atlantics, for which the drawings were prepared in 1909. For some unknown reason they did not become V1 as they should have done if standard NER practice had been followed.

The Raven Pacifics carried 'Class 4-6-2'. This also appeared on the Gresley Pacifics after their first overhaul at Darlington, but this practice ceased after they were transferred to Doncaster for maintenance in 1930. In 1938 all LNER locomotive works commenced to put the LNER class on the buffer beam, as Darlington works had been doing since 1932.

Two sections of the main line as we know it today are not the original route. Between Shaftholme Junction and Chaloner Whin Junction (York), and Ferryhill and Gateshead, the present route is an improvement on the original.

From Shaftholme Junction the original route was over the Lancashire & Yorkshire Railway to Knottingley, where the York & North Midland was joined to reach George Hudson's Altofts Junction (Normanton) to York line at Burton Salmon.

From Ferryhill the 'old main line' ran via Shincliffe, Leamside, Penshaw and Washington, to Gateshead. The section between Washington and Gateshead originally went via Brockley Whins (now Boldon Colliery), but a cut-off line from Washington to Pelaw was opened in 1850 and this continued in use until through running from Gateshead to Ferryhill via Durham became possible in January 1872. Even so, the Team Valley route did not immediately achieve main-line status and some East Coast expresses continued to run via the 'old main line'.

However, since the Knottingley and Leamside routes lost their regular main line traffic they have been extremely useful as alternative routes when the main line has been blocked by engineering work or accident.

Other routes which have been used frequently for diversions off the main line are:

York-Starbeck-Ripon-Northallerton*
Darlington-Bishop Auckland-Durham*
Northallerton or Geneva curve (Darlington)-Eaglescliffe- Stockton-Stillington-Ferryhill
Low Fell-Dunston-Scotswood-Newcastle
Newcastle-Backworth-Morpeth
Newcastle-South Gosforth-Benton-Forest Hall
Tweedmouth-Kelso-Galashiels-Edinburgh*
These routes are no longer available.

Although the flow of traffic on the main line is north and south there is a flow from north-east to south-west (Newcastle-Bristol) and north-east to west (Newcastle-Liverpool). Trains on these services use the North Eastern part of the main line between Newcastle and York.

Two secondary routes, one of which is now closed, have also been involved in main-line workings: Newcastle-Sunderland-West Hartlepool-Stockton-Northallerton, which is still open; and Northallerton-Ripon-Harrogate-Leeds, which is now closed between Northallerton and Harrogate. A combination of these two routes was used by some Newcastle-Liverpool trains, and the Northallerton-Leeds section was also used by the Pullman trains, which reversed at Leeds (Central) and then ran via Wakefield (Westgate) to rejoin the main line at Doncaster. The engines working these trains were from the Main Line links and thus were regularly 4-4-2s, 4-6-2s or 2-6-2s.

The 44.1mile section of the main line between York and Darlington has long been famous as a high-speed stretch. For years prior to World War I it was one of the few lines where trains were timed at an average speed of more than 60mph. Now diesel-hauled trains regularly traverse the line at 100mph and over. Between the end of World War I and the Grouping the North Eastern had plans to electrify the main line between York and Newcastle and also the Northallerton-Stockton-Ferryhill loop, but unfortunately this did not reach fruition. If it had come off this would have been the country's outstanding main line and might have prompted main-line electrification on a large scale long before the West Coast line was electrified half a century later. It remains to be seen if the East Coast line will be electrified some 60 years after conversion was first proposed.

1925-1929

This narrative commences at a time of great change in the main motive power of the East Coast route. Twenty Gresley Pacifics had just been distributed between the sheds responsible for working the principal trains over the 205 miles between York and Edinburgh, displacing to some extent the North Eastern Atlantics which had performed such good work since 1903. However, there was still plenty of work for the four varieties of Atlantics and the 72 engines remained on main-line duties, although not on the main expresses: they were used on semi-fasts, excursions, reliefs, and braked goods – mainly fish and meat – and often in pairs if a Pacific was not available. In addition there were five Raven Pacifics.

The allocation of the Gresley and Raven engines was:

Edinburgh (Haymarket) A1 Nos 2563-7
Gateshead A1 Nos 2568-77, A2 Nos 2400-4
Heaton A1 Nos 2578-82

It will be noted that there were no Pacifics at York in spite of its eminence as a railway centre. Thus Heaton and Gateshead were responsible for working from Newcastle northwards to Edinburgh and southwards to York. The Edinburgh engines worked south to Newcastle in a link based on the old-established practice of having North Eastern engines and men out-stationed at Edinburgh solely for working to Newcastle; this had come about as early as 1869, but although the practice had ceased for a period in the last decade of the 19th century (due to dis-satisfaction by the North British Railway) the North Eastern workings had continued up to the Grouping of 1 January 1923. Thus, except for a period in the very early days of the LNER when North British Atlantics worked through from Edinburgh to Newcastle on the Pullman trains and one or two other workings, North British passenger engines had never regularly penetrated south of Berwick.

The introduction of the Gresley Pacifics to Haymarket shed and the integration of North Eastern men into the Southern Scottish Area meant that for the first time a regular link, Scottish-based, could be formed of Edinburgh men for the Newcastle workings, although at first the North Eastern men predominated as they knew the road south of Berwick, and also the method of working. Later, as the former North Eastern men retired the Newcastle link became a true Scottish working and Haymarket men, previously used to going only as far as Glasgow, Perth, or Dundee, found themselves running through to Kings Cross, although only as passengers on the southern half of the non-stop 'Flying Scotsman', which they had manned as far as the halfway point.

At first the Gresley Pacifics were treated as the North Eastern Atlantics had been – usually with two sets of men to an engine, with the Gateshead and Heaton engines running perhaps a return trip to Edinburgh with one set, and a return trip to York with the other, in each 24 hours, giving a total daily mileage of 410. Although this was quite a respectable figure it did not apply to all the engines as some made only one return trip to Edinburgh (250 miles) or York (160 miles) in each 24 hours. The Edinburgh engines normally performed one return trip to Newcastle each day (250 miles). Thus it was obvious that such large engines should be capable of more intensive utilisation, both technically and economically. The need for improvement of the passenger services in the 1920s, coupled with the need for greater use of the Pacifics, led to the non-stop Kings Cross-Newcastle working in 1927 and the non-stop Kings Cross-Edinburgh working in the following year. From these developed the 'Silver Jubilee' (1935) and 'Coronation' (1937) expresses – producing the peak of LNER locomotive performance which lasted until the outbreak of war in September 1939.

Almost without exception the Great Northern Railway had worked the East Coast services between Doncaster and York, and the North Eastern the local trains. However, a precedent was created in 1903 when the North Eastern worked the up and down 'Scotsman' to and from Doncaster with York engines and men, although the trains did not stop at York in either direction. Over the years the working was frequently modified until, in the summer of 1922, Gateshead men were working the 8.0am Newcastle-Kings Cross as far as Doncaster, returning at 1.3pm from Doncaster, not stopping at York. Thus after the Grouping it was a small step to extend former NER workings a further 51 miles to Grantham, and this was put into force for the summer of 1923, with a GN conductor from Selby on the 8.0am from Newcastle.

In the Gateshead link responsible for this working was Driver Tom Blades, who worked the Raven Pacific No 2400 on its trials against a Gresley Pacific on the Great Northern main line. His fireman at the time was Charlie Fisher, later to become a well-known NE Region locomotive inspector. Charlie recounts the following story of one of their exploits:

'Having received a letter from HQ, issued to each set of men on the East Coast expresses, as to the importance of making every effort to maintain running times on these trains, we were out to show what we could do. It was a Monday morning when we received the letter and Tom Blades and I were 8.0am Newcastle, Darlington, and Selby to Grantham, arrive 11.28am — a most important business train for London.

'That morning we had Z No 2196 in spanking condition. All was going well, but with the double fire-door blinder down and running easy after Aycliffe, Tom eased the regulator and I noticed that the steam pressure gauge did not move. I immediately lifted the blinder, looked into the firebox, and there was the front half of the firebars down and the fire into the ashpan. Blades calmly whistled for a fresh engine at Darlington passing Low Beaumont Hill, and again at Springfield.

'We took three minutes longer than booked at Darlington, changing 2196 for D20 4-4-0 No 725. The latter had been out all night on standby pilot and the coal, all small, was well back in the tender. Needless to say, the outlook was gloomy! However, off from Darlington three minutes late, with not a word spoken. Passing Eryholme Tom opened 725's regulator fully and notched up to one from the centre. I was firing with all the skill I knew, fortunately being used to small coal through

having fired at Blaydon, putting the coal around the box pepper-and-salt fashion, little and often. To my delight 725 stood up and we passed York on time, with still no remarks from Tom.

'We arrived at Selby at 10.0am for a two-minute stop and a GN conductor stepped on to conduct us between Doncaster and Grantham, although we didn't really require him as we had just returned from the London trials. At Selby Blades looked round the engine and soon shouted to ask if we could see a piece of wood and some rope anywhere about. Of course there was nothing. Then we were whistled away. Tom shouted that it was alright and off we went, full belt as before. The GN driver and I hadn't a clue as to why Tom wanted the wood and rope. We arrived at Grantham at 11.28am, on time, and I will never forget the tall figure of Tom Blades standing up, a slight flush on his face, when I asked what he wanted the items for at Selby. "I wonder what the big-end is like", he said calmly. "You see, we had lost the right big-end key before Selby". What a shock for me!

'Had Tom closed the regulator completely at any time before coming to a stand at Grantham we would most certainly have had the right cylinder cover broken to pieces and the piston damaged. We should also have had to have a fresh engine, causing delay. But thanks to Tom's skill all this was avoided.'

This, therefore, was the sort of working taken over by the Gresley Pacifics soon after they arrived

Gateshead Main Line No 1

	arr	dep	
Newcastle	–	4.43am	(10-35pm ex-KX)
Edinburgh	7.30am	10.0am	'Flying Scotsman'
Newcastle	12.33pm	12.40pm	do
York	2.24pm	5.3pm	(1.15pm ex-KX)
Newcastle	6.53pm	–	

Gateshead Main Line No 2

Newcastle	–	11.17am	(8.55am Leeds–Glasgow)
Edinburgh	1.43pm	5.12pm	(4.0pm Glasgow-Leeds)
Newcastle	7.56pm	8.5pm	do
York	9.44pm	11.55pm	Express goods
Forth	3.37am	–	

Gateshead Main Line No 3

Newcastle	–	12.23pm	(10.5am ex York)
Edinburgh	3.35pm	5.27pm	(Aberdeen fish)
Newcastle	8.19pm	8.27pm	do
York	10.0pm	1.15am	Express goods
Heaton	4.35am	–	

at Gateshead. It developed into such diagrams as listed in the table opposite.

Thus if a locomotive could complete these diagrams, involving 410 miles a day, it was feasible for it to run the 392.7 miles from London to Edinburgh. But could it be done non-stop?

The first step in this direction came on 11 July 1927 when Kings Cross and Gateshead engines and men commenced working the non-stop 9.50am Kings Cross to Newcastle. Kings Cross used A1 Pacifics Nos 2552 *Sansovino*, 4474 *Victor Wild*, and 4475 *Flying Fox*, and Gateshead Nos 2569 *Gladiateur* and 2575 *Galopin*. The working was complicated by the fact that the train did not run on Tuesdays and Wednesdays, but the up balancing working at 9.30am from Newcastle ran each day. Thus Kings Cross engines and men worked the 9.50am down on Mondays and Fridays and the 9.30am up on Tuesdays and Saturdays, whilst Gateshead worked the 9.50am down on Thursdays and Saturdays and the 9.30am up on Wednesdays and Fridays. On Mondays the 9.30am ex-Newcastle was worked by Gateshead men to York, with Doncaster men forward to Kings Cross, and on Thursdays by York men to York and Doncaster men to Kings Cross.

This well publicised non-stop working was first covered on Monday 11 July by Driver Pibworth of Kings Cross with No 4475 *Flying Fox*, and the second on Thursday 14 July by Tom Blades of Gateshead with No 2569 *Gladiateur*. Fireman to Blades at this time was W. Morris and the other Gateshead crews were: Driver J. C. Smith and Fireman Bambra; Driver R. S. More and Fireman S. Silson; and Driver J. G. Eltringham and Fireman J. Slinger. On the inaugural run the train arrived at Newcastle on time, but on the Thursday it was six minutes early into Newcastle. A conductor was carried throughout on each trip – a GN man with the North Eastern Area crew for the London-Grantham section, and a NE man with the Southern Area crew for the York-Newcastle section. Perhaps the greatest effect of this 268 miles non-stop run was the enormous publicity it generated – helped, no doubt, by the LNER Publicity Department.

At this time there was keen rivalry between the LMS and the LNER and the former now attempted to steal the East Coast's thunder by making one-off non-stop runs to Glasgow and Edinburgh. These were performed after the LNER had announced that from 1 May 1928 it was to run the up and down 'Flying Scotsman' trains non-stop between London and Edinburgh *daily*! The Gresley Pacifics were already equipped with large eight-wheel tenders and water could be picked up at six sets of water troughs en route, but it was the long distance for one crew that posed the greatest problem.

As is well known this was overcome by providing corridor tenders, so that the first crew could be relieved by another crew at the mid-way point of the journey near Tollerton, north of York. The third-class compartment nearest the engine in the leading coach was reserved for the footplate crews. They were provided with a free meal from the restaurant car, the second crew before they passed through the tender to take over for the second half of the journey, and the first crew after they had completed their half of the trip and been relieved.

The first corridor tenders, which were completed at Doncaster works in 50 days from the issue of the instructions and drawings, were based on the standard eight-wheel tenders fitted to the Gresley Pacifics, but they presented a smoother appearance with the absence of coal rails along each side. The 5ft-high corridor ran along the right-hand side of the tender, illuminated from the front by a window in the door, and from the rear by a porthole in the top corner of the backplate.

This innovation, and the fact that the trains were to run almost 393 miles non-stop six days a week for the duration of the summer timetable, created far more public interest than the mere 268 miles on the 9.50am down in 1927, and the publicity value was enormous. The economics of the working were probably not too satisfactory – it must have been difficult to find each day some 200 passengers all wishing to travel from London to Edinburgh at 10.0am! There was also the problem of ensuring that no stop signal was against the train throughout the whole of the journey, for the LNER tried most zealously to ensure that the non-stop really was non-stop.

Discussion about working the non-stop between London and Edinburgh had originated in 1927. Gresley's first concern was over the water supplies, particularly in running between Wiske Moor and Lucker, the only two sets of troughs north of Doncaster. These had been sited at a time when all main-line trains changed engines at York and Newcastle and thus commenced their journeys with a full tank. South of Doncaster water was no problem, as there were four sets of troughs, but Bawtry to Wiske Moor was 76 miles, Wiske Moor to Lucker 98 miles, and Lucker to Edinburgh 73 miles.

In January 1928 trials were held with No 2582 *Sir Hugo* on a 350ton train and the maximum water pick up was 1,914gallons. Air vents in the water space were required to allow the water to fill the tank the last 8in or 10in, and improved valves were to be fitted at Wiske Moor troughs to get them replenished more quickly. Even so it was found that if a train running immediately ahead of the non-stop picked up water there was not enough in the troughs for the 'Scotsman', which occasionally had to make a special stop for water. Consequently an instruction was issued that trains in front of the 'Scotsman' should not pick up water unless it was absolutely essential.

On 10 February 1928 No 2568 *Sceptre*, with a 450ton special train, worked a trial non-stop run from York to Edinburgh with Driver Eltringham, accompanied by Inspector Gill. The time allowed for the 205miles was 258minutes. Wiske Moor troughs, with the new valves, provided 2,387gallons of water, and 2,545gallons were picked up at Lucker, giving a total consumption of 6,440gallons at 31.5gallons per mile. On this basis it was considered quite feasible to run non-stop from London to Edinburgh.

Oil supplies were also causing a small problem, but this was overcome by providing larger oil cups, and Wakefield lubricators with a larger oil capacity than the Detroit pattern already fitted.

In February 1928 the question of manning the engines was laid before the various Locomotive Running Superintendents. It is of note that at this time the LNER intended to run not only the 10.0am from London and the 10.0am from Edinburgh non-stop, but also two night trains, the 11.10pm from Kings Cross and the 10.50pm from Edinburgh. Three manning alternatives were put forward:

(A) Southern Area and North Eastern Area men on day trains Southern Area and Scottish Area men on night trains
(B) Southern Area and Scottish Area men on all trains
(C) Southern Area and North Eastern Area men on all trains

Scheme A was the most costly and Scheme C the cheapest.

However, it was decided eventually to run only the day trains non-stop, so a fresh look had to be taken at the question, especially when the General Manager expressed the view that the crews should be provided by all three Areas. Eventually, in March 1928, the Scottish Area Running Superintendent put forward the rosters that were adopted. They were complicated by the fact that the North Eastern Area men from Gateshead were to be used, and yet the trains, being non-stop in both directions, did not call at Newcastle to allow

crews to be changed. Consequently Gateshead men worked from Newcastle to Edinburgh one day, lodged overnight at Edinburgh, worked the up non-stop as far as Tollerton, continued as passengers to London, lodged overnight in London, travelled as passengers on the non-stop as far as Tollerton and then worked it to Edinburgh, lodged overnight in Edinburgh, and returned home on the fourth day.

Obviously it would have been simpler to have worked the trains solely with London and Edinburgh men (as was eventually done after World War II). But as North Eastern men had been responsible for the York-Edinburgh section for almost 60 years it was probably felt that friction would develop if they had been left out.

In the meantime the Assistant Chief Mechanical Engineer located at Darlington, A. C. Stamer, had been asked to suggest suitable engines to work from the Edinburgh end. He picked Nos 2569 *Gladiateur*, 2573 *Harvester* and 2580 *Shotover*. All had just been fitted with long travel valves, and in addition Nos 2573 and 2580 had received boilers working at 220lb/sq in against the original 180lb. The scheme was to use one of these engines with a Scottish Area crew on the footplate north of Tollerton, and a London crew south of Tollerton. The opposite working was with a Kings Cross engine, again with a London crew south of Tollerton but with a Gateshead crew from Tollerton to Edinburgh.

On the eventful day, 1 May 1928, the 10.0am from Kings Cross was worked by No 4472 *Flying Scotsman*, with Driver Pibworth and Fireman Goddard of Kings Cross, relieved by Driver Blades and Fireman Morris of Gateshead, and the 10.0am from Edinburgh by Driver Henderson and Fireman McKenzie of Haymarket, relieved by Driver Day and Fireman Gray of Kings Cross. Other Gateshead crews involved were Drivers H. Pennington, J. Gascoigne, J. W. Halford, J. C. Smith, and J. G. Eltringham, with Firemen J. Ridley, J. J. Williams, J. F. Cairn, J. Bambra, and J. Slinger respectively.

The crews were paid on a mileage basis of 200 miles for the half journey, together with an *ex-gratia* payment of one day's pay, so that the Gateshead drivers were receiving more than £27 a fortnight, and the firemen more than £21. In addition they received a lodging allowance of £3 15s 11d a fortnight – a large amount for footplate crews in the 1920s!

The inaugural down train had a load of 12 coaches with a tare load of 386tons and arrived at Edinburgh at 6.2pm, six minutes early by the working time of 6.8pm, although the public time remained at the standard 6.15pm. In the up direction *Shotover* had 10 coaches, 323tons tare, and arrived at Kings Cross one minute early at 6.14pm; in this direction the public and working times were the same. One of the tender bearings on No 4472 tended to run hot on the down trip, but it was got ready in time to work up the next day, although for the second trip Kings Cross provided No 2546 *Donovan,* with No 4472 fit again to take the third Kings Cross trip on the fifth day. No 2580 worked all five up and down trips in the first week, gaining 32 minutes on booked time, but it must be admitted that the timing was generous. The time allowed for the 233miles from Shaftholme Junction to Edinburgh was the same – 306 minutes – whether running non-stop or whether stops totalling 20 minutes were made at York, Newcastle and Berwick!

Unfortunately the 19th century agreement between the East Coast and West Coast companies restricted the times of the day trains to 8¼ hours by both routes, although night trains via the East Coast could reach Edinburgh in 7¾ hours, and via West Coast could make Glasgow in 8 hours.

A sidelight of the non-stop working was the introduction of a headboard on No 2580 on the first up train. This displayed the name of the train 'Flying Scotsman' in black letters on a white background, and the board was carried on the top centre lamp-bracket. The board was a modification of a type of headboard/destination board used in Scotland for some years, and it created such a favourable impression that a similar board was soon prepared for use on the Kings Cross engine on the opposite working. This device was then adopted for use on all other LNER named trains.

The allocation of three North Eastern Area Pacifics to the non-stop working left Gateshead short of engines, as they received only No 2565 *Merry Hampton* in exchange, and this engine did not have Westinghouse brake equipment, which was still used in the Area. Thus there was pressure to get back the Westinghouse-fitted engines from Haymarket and this was backed by the Scottish Area's wish to use their own engines on the non-stop, particularly Nos 2563 *William Whitelaw* and 2564 *Knight of the Thistle.* Gresley was approached on this point on 7 May 1928 and gave permission, whereupon a start was made on preparing Nos 2563 and 2564. This involved transferring the corridor tenders off Nos 2569 and 2573 and the two North Eastern Area engines were then returned to Gateshead, although their Westinghouse brake gear was still inoperative as they were returned with the vacuum-braked

tenders off Nos 2563 and 2564. Arrangements then had to be made to get the two Westinghouse-fitted tenders sent from Doncaster to Darlington so that Nos 2569 and 2573 could pay a quick visit to North Road to regain their original tenders. *Shotover* was retained in Scotland until the non-stop working ceased on 22 September 1928: the working was, however, resumed for each subsequent summer up to and including 1939.

In July 1927 No 4480 *Enterprise,* a Southern Area engine, was rebuilt with a 220lb boiler and three North Eastern Area engines were similarly treated in 1928, No 2573 *Harvester* in April, No 2578 *Bayardo* in May, and No 2580 *Shotover* in February. All were fitted with long travel valves at the same time, although retaining 20in diameter cylinders, and reclassified A3. All subsequent unstreamlined Gresley Pacifics were turned out with this type of boiler and the remaining 48 were rebuilt to correspond, although this took until December 1948 to accomplish. Ten new engines built with 220lb boilers appeared from Doncaster in 1928/9, Nos 2743-52, but none were allocated to the North Eastern Area, although Nos 2743/4/6/7/ 50/1/2 worked into the Area from the Southern Area. The other three, Nos 2745/8/9, settled down to many years' work over the Waverley route between Carlisle and Edinburgh, but did very occasionally appear at Newcastle.

The year 1927 saw the introduction of the D49 'Shire' class 4-4-0 engines, of which the first, No 234 *Yorkshire,* was placed in traffic in October. This was Gresley's only design of 4-4-0 built for the LNER and it used the same boiler as the contemporary J39 0-6-0 engines, both of which types originated at Darlington. The new 4-4-0 engines had three cylinders with piston valves operated by Gresley's conjugated valve gear, although after 20 of this type had been built a change was made to oscillating cam-operated poppet valves and six of this pattern were built. Next came a batch of eight engines to the original design, concurrently with two rotary cam poppet-valve engines, making a total of 36 engines built between October 1927 and June 1929. Of these, 13 were allocated to the North Eastern Area and 23 to the Scottish Area. Those in England were divided between York (6) and Leeds (7): York's allocation was Nos 320/2/7/35/6/52 and at Leeds were Nos 234/6/45/51/3/6 and 318. Two Leeds engines, Nos 253 and 256, were exchanged for Nos 320 and 322 of York in July 1928, and No 245 was on loan to Kings Cross from September 1928 to April 1929.

With a fleet of Atlantic engines, and with the main East Coast trains worked by other sheds, York did not use its D49s on main line trains to any great extent. Certainly they operated south to Grantham and north to Newcastle, but their main work was done on the secondary lines radiating from York to Scarborough, Leeds, Hull, and Sheffield. On the other hand, Leeds Neville Hill regularly used D49 engines on their top turns to Newcastle. These trains had for some years been worked by a fleet of North Eastern Atlantics stationed at Leeds and in 1927 these were Nos 718/29,2201/2/3/6/7/10. Soon after the arrival of the D49 engines Nos 718/29 and 2207 were displaced to Tweedmouth and Nos 2201/2/3/6 to Gateshead: the remaining C7 (No. 2210) went to Heaton in June 1929.

The top main-line turn for the new D49 engines was the 8.55am Leeds to Glasgow via York, which the Neville Hill engine worked as far as Newcastle, returning on the 1.5pm Newcastle-York and the 3.30pm York-Leeds (a train which originated at Scarborough). Another Leeds working for very many years was the morning Liverpool (Lime Street) to Newcastle train, taken over at Leeds New by a D49, and the return at 4.17pm from Newcastle. Although a Leeds top link working, both these trains ran via Wetherby, Harrogate, Ripon, Northallerton, Stockton, West Hartlepool and Sunderland.

The rostered formation for the ex-LNWR corridor set used on this Liverpool-Newcastle service on certain days was a brake third at each end, with a first and three thirds between, providing 36 first-class seats and 200 third-class. The weight of the set empty was 170tons. At Leeds a third-class kitchen car and an open first were attached, adding 70tons to the load and providing extra seating accommodation for 30 third-class and 36 first-class passengers respectively; these two vehicles were detached at Leeds on the return journey. This set rotated with a similar LMS set making one Liverpool-Newcastle or Newcastle-Liverpool journey daily, and with an LNER set also making one trip daily. Thus the 11.15am from Leeds and the 4.17pm from Newcastle had one LMS set on Mondays and Thursdays, the second LMS set on Wednesdays and Saturdays, and the LNER set on Tuesdays and Fridays. The LNER set, although of the same basic composition, was nominally 14tons heavier but provided an additional 40 third-class seats: an additional corridor third was added on Saturdays in summer.

Thus on the days the LNER set was rostered the Leeds D49 was faced with 254tons tare over the gradients between Leeds and Wetherby, although these were actually worse in the up direction when there was a climb of between 1 in 68 and 1 in 90 for some 5½ miles, from Collingham Bridge to Scholes. I remember many a pleasant journey over this route when I joined the 4.17pm ex Newcastle at Harrogate or Ripon, with the D49 blasting away as it swung round the curves, then dropping down to Cross Gates, checking over the junction on to the Hull/York line, and making a final gallop downhill to Neville Hill before the brakes went hard on to negotiate the junctions and to thread the deep cutting to Marsh Lane. A cautious run over the two-track viaduct spanning some of the less salubrious parts of Leeds, then we were at a stand under the Mansard roof of Leeds New (later City) station, with the 'Wessie' engine blowing off at the west end ready to take over on the next stage to Huddersfield and Manchester.

From the Edinburgh end D49 engines did occasionally work south to Newcastle, but only at times of pressure as they were not regularly rostered for the top East Coast jobs.

Pullman cars had been used by the East Coast companies in the nineteenth century, but there were only three cars and of these one was destroyed in the Manor House collision of 1892, whilst the other two were divided between the NER and GNR when they had become unfit for East Coast service. With the formation of the LNER a number of Pullman cars which had been in use on the Great Eastern Railway became available and it was decided to try Pullman trains on services out of Kings Cross. As early as 9 July 1923 the 'Harrogate Pullman' commenced running to Newcastle via Leeds (Central) and Harrogate, and on 12 July 1925 this service was extended to Edinburgh. With the commencement of the winter timetable on 21 September 1925 a second train started running, known as the 'West Riding Pullman', and this ran to Leeds (with a portion for Bradford, and later Halifax), although the up train started its journey at Harrogate. Now that the new Pullman served Leeds it was decided to route the 'Harrogate Pullman' via Shaftholme Junction, Knottingley, Church Fenton and Tadcaster to Harrogate, with Kings Cross engines working through to Harrogate. In those early years the Pullman services were covered by former Great Central B3 4-6-0s and D11 4-4-0s, together with ex-Great Northern Atlantics. North of Harrogate the Pullmans were normally worked by North Eastern Atlantics and Raven and Gresley Pacifics, although for a short while North British Atlantics appeared from the Edinburgh end as far as Newcastle.

On the day the non-stop 'Flying Scotsman' commenced running, 1 May 1928, further changes were made to the Pullman services. The 'Harrogate Pullman' reverted to its original route via Leeds (Central) and at the same time was extended to Glasgow and renamed the 'Queen of Scots'. The 'West Riding Pullman' was extended to Harrogate and Newcastle, but retained its original name. Henceforward the Pullman services were little changed, apart from acceleration, until 1935 and 1937, when the introduction of the 'Silver Jubilee' and 'Coronation' respectively brought about alterations.

Main-line goods workings in the five years under review were handled by North Eastern 0-6-0 engines of Classes J26 and J27, and Q5, Q6 and Q7 0-8-0s, with the various classes of 4-6-0s on the faster trains, and increasing participation by the new J39 0-6-0s and K3 2-6-0s, although the quantity available up to 1929 – 12 J39 and 10 K3 – was not sufficient to make any significant change, and none were actually stationed at main-line sheds at first. However, it must be remembered that a number of the top passenger diagrams involved balancing working of a fitted goods, fish or meat train, in one direction.

The first 12 J39 0-6-0s were allocated to the North Eastern Area when they were built in 1926, allowing a similar number of superheated J27 0-6-0s to be transferred to the Great Eastern section. The J39s were allocated to Newport (6); West Hartlepool (3); and Hull Dairycoates (3). However, in November 1927 the three Hull engines, Nos 1451, 1452 and 1454, were required at Blaydon for Carlisle services and these displaced two K3s from Blaydon, Nos 17 and 28, to York, where they joined Nos 39, 52 and 53 on services radiating from the city.

The NER had tried a Weir feed-water-heater on a Class S2 4-6-0 and in February 1926 C7 Atlantic No 2163 was fitted with one of the Dabeg pattern; dynamometer car trials followed between York and Grantham. Early in 1928 Nos 728 and 2206 of the same class were fitted with equipment of the ACFI pattern and in August 1928 No 2206 was tested using the dynamometer car. However, the report by the Chief Test Inspector stated that no conclusive results had been obtained and that little advantage could be expected. This he put down to the intensive use of engines and went on:

'When men are moved about from one engine to another, as they are under present conditions, they lose interest and we might as well resign ourselves to the fact that they will not use these appliances if they can help it, especially if they are complicated, as is the case with the majority of these fittings. Further than this they are not looked on favourably at the Running Sheds as the repair staff, cut down in numbers in the interests of economy, have only time to execute repairs to

essentials, and whilst speaking solely as an engineer I think these devices ingenious I fear that having regard to human nature we shall be disappointed if we expect to reap any advantage from their use'.

Further trials with No 2206 were carried out in April and May 1929, and although small savings were made in coal and water it was doubtful if these could be maintained with the locomotive in general use. Certainly there was little similarity between working with the dynamometer car behind the tender and a locomotive inspector on the footplate breathing down the driver's neck, on an engine specially prepared, and the everyday hurly-burly of running shed and footplate work.

In spite of the Test Inspector's report Gresley Pacifics Nos 2576 (A1) and 2580 (A3) were also fitted with ACFI feed-water-heaters in August and July 1929 respectively, but apart from ruining the appearance of the engines the equipment seems to have been of little value and Darlington Works turned its attention to exhaust injectors. Thus C7 No 2171 was tried between York and Grantham in June 1929 with a Davies & Metcalfe pattern injector, but here again the results were inconclusive; further trials were carried out in September 1929.

In North Eastern days the various Atlantic classes were expected to run 85,000 miles between general overhaul, but the LNER reduced this to 75,000 for C7 engines, 65,000 for C6, and 60,000 for C8. The Raven and Gresley Pacifics were also 'shopped' at Darlington at around 75,000 miles, but for some reason the Gresley Pacifics in the Southern and Scottish Areas were sent to works at 5,000 miles less. Until March 1930 Nos 2568-82 were overhauled at Darlington Works and thus acquired 'CLASS 4-6-2' on their front buffer beams; this, together with the Westinghouse pumps on the right-hand side of the engine, made the North Eastern Area engines distinctive.

The 1920s were marred by three serious accidents on the main line: the deliberate derailment of No 2565 *Merry Hampton* at Cramlington on 10 May 1926, and the collisions at Darlington in 1928 and 1929. The Cramlington incident took place during the General Strike when a rail was loosened (and probably removed) by strikers. *Merry Hampton* was working the 10.0am from Edinburgh, consisting of nine bogie vehicles and a triplet kitchen car set. The engine fell over on to its left-hand side, as did the leading coach, but fortunately the train was travelling slowly as it had just stopped to pick up a volunteer platelayer gang. Before they joined the train they had warned the driver that there was an antagonistic crowd on the lineside ahead. Driver R. Sheddon, a former North

British driver, was at the regulator and as he did not know the road south of Berwick he had been joined at Berwick by a North Eastern conductor; two volunteer firemen were also on the footplate. Driver Sheddon was one of the Haymarket drivers chosen for the non-stop 'Flying Scotsman' working in 1928. After the engine and part of the train had been derailed, and as the passengers were being helped out of the coaches, the nearby crowd laughed and jeered!

The first Darlington accident occurred at the south end of Bank Top station on the late evening of 27 June 1928. An up parcels train was carrying out shunting operations when the engine, B16 No 2369, fouled the down main line which passes outside the station. Rapidly approaching was an excursion returning from Scarborough to Newcastle behind C7 No 2164 and this collided head-on with the B16, which was pushed back 185ft. The C7 was badly damaged at the front end and fell over on to its left-hand side, but the crews of both engines escaped death. The greatest damage was, however, to some of the coaches, which were badly telescoped. Twenty-five passengers were killed, many of them women from one village in County Durham, Hetton-le-Hole, who had been to Scarborough on a day's outing. Both engines were repaired at Darlington Works and put back to traffic; in fact the Atlantic, No 2164, was the last North Eastern Atlantic to run and it was not withdrawn until December 1948.

The second Darlington collision took place at the opposite end of Bank Top station some nine months later, on 9 March 1929. On this occasion an engine standing on the main line was forgotten by the signalman and the driver omitted to send his fireman to the signalbox to carry out Rule 55. The signalman accepted and pulled off for an up express with C7 No 2205 to enter the station and as it did so it collided at about 10mph with D23 4-4-0 No 274. The 4-4-0 was pushed back some 150ft and derailed, and the C7 fell over on to its right-hand side. A guard in the front van of the express was killed. After being repaired at North Road Works

and put back to traffic No 2205, together with Nos 2165, 2202 and 2203 of the same class, was transferred to Tweedmouth on 9 June 1930 to replace Nos 295, 696, 699 and 700 of Class C6.

Tweedmouth shed provided engines for semi-fast passenger trains to Edinburgh and Newcastle, but more importantly it supplied engines to work fitted goods trains between Tweedmouth and Newcastle.

In 1926 up braked fish and meat trains – 10.40am Meat Aberdeen-Kings Cross; 1.10pm, 1.45pm, and 2.10pm Fish Aberdeen-Kings Cross; 12 noon Fish Mallaig-Kings Cross; and 6.18pm Fish Heaton-Kings Cross – could be worked through the North Eastern Area by C7 Atlantic engines hauling a maximum load of 300tons. A pilot could be taken if this load was exceeded, subject to a maximum of 42 wagons (including brake-van). Pacific engines on such trains, according to instructions issued in February 1927, could take up to 400tons, but no piloting was allowed unless the engine became defective after leaving the shed! However, in 1933 this loading was increased to 500tons for a Pacific and 385tons for an Atlantic if the train ran at 40mph instead of 50mph.

An example of the higher speed booking was the 6.53 Fish from Newcastle (6.16pm from Heaton) which in 1934 was allowed 101 minutes for the 80.1 miles between Newcastle and York, or only two minutes more than some passenger trains also booked non-stop over the same distance. These trains were shown in the Working Timetable as: 'Will take precedence over all trains except East Coast passenger trains'.

Above right: Class A1 4-6-2 No. 2574 *St. Frusquin* arriving at Leeds New station, west end, on a train from Newcastle via Harrogate./*S. Ellingworth*

Right: Class Z 4-4-2 (LNER C7) No. 706 leaving York for Newcastle, with the NER dynamometer car as the leading vehicle./*C. Ord*

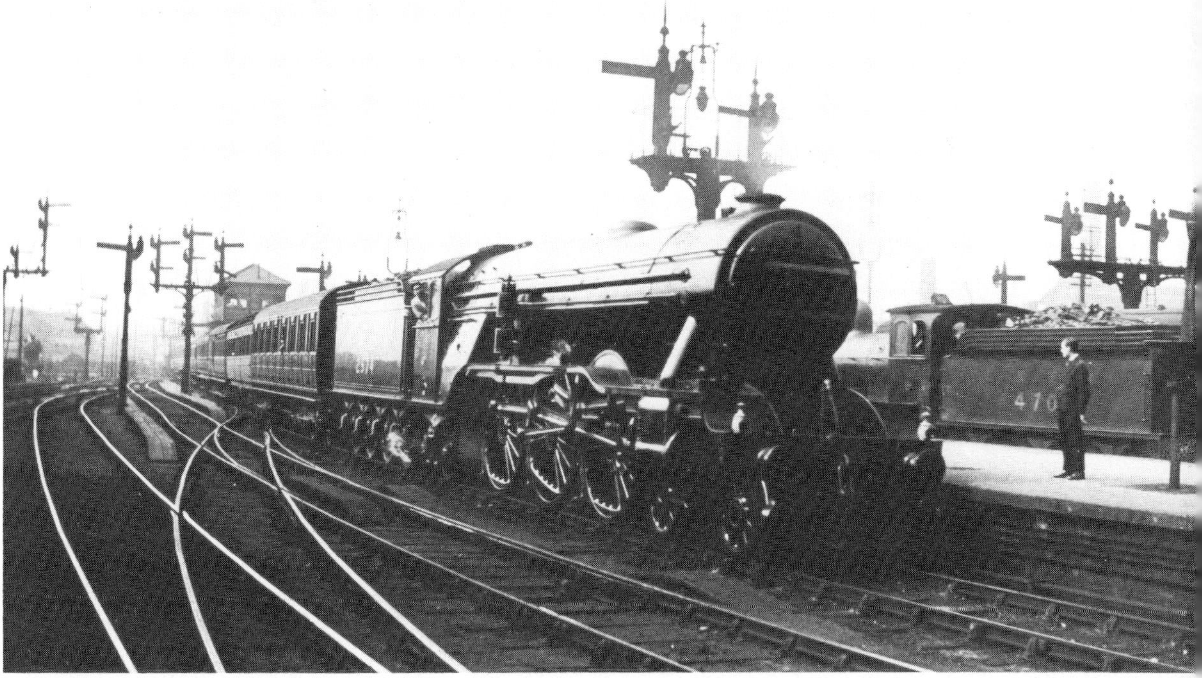

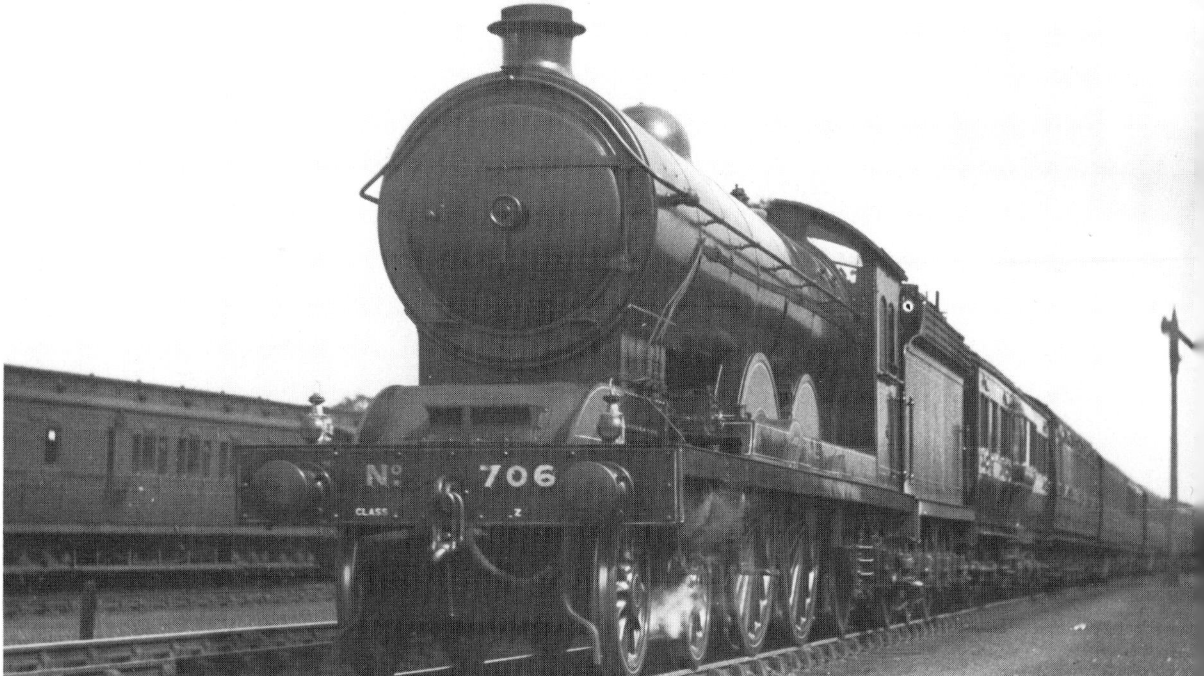
No 706
CLASS Z

Below: Class Z 4-4-2 No. 719 piloting Class V/09 4-4-2 No. 698 on an up express at Chester Moor Colliery 22 August 1926. */H. G. W. Household*

Bottom: Class D20 4-4-0 No. 1210 passing Craigentinny on a Berwick slow./*H. L. Salmon*

Right: Class B13 4-6-0 No. 753 (NER Class S) passing Hett Mill box – one of the few level crossings between York and Newcastle – on a down goods on 3 September 1926./*H. G. W. Household*

Below right: Class J26 (NER Class P2) 0-6-0 No. 1671 at York on an up goods./*H. L. Salmon*

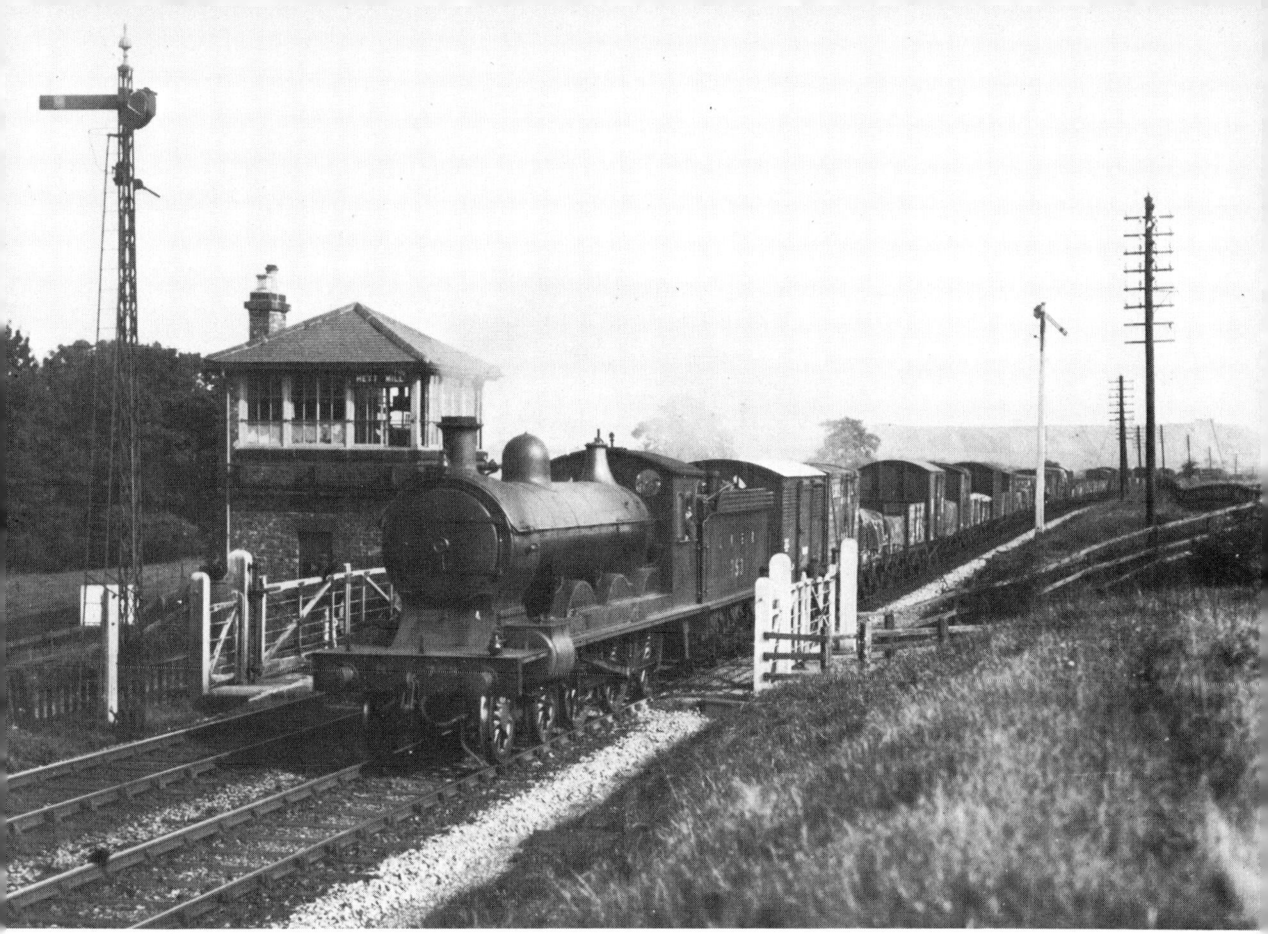

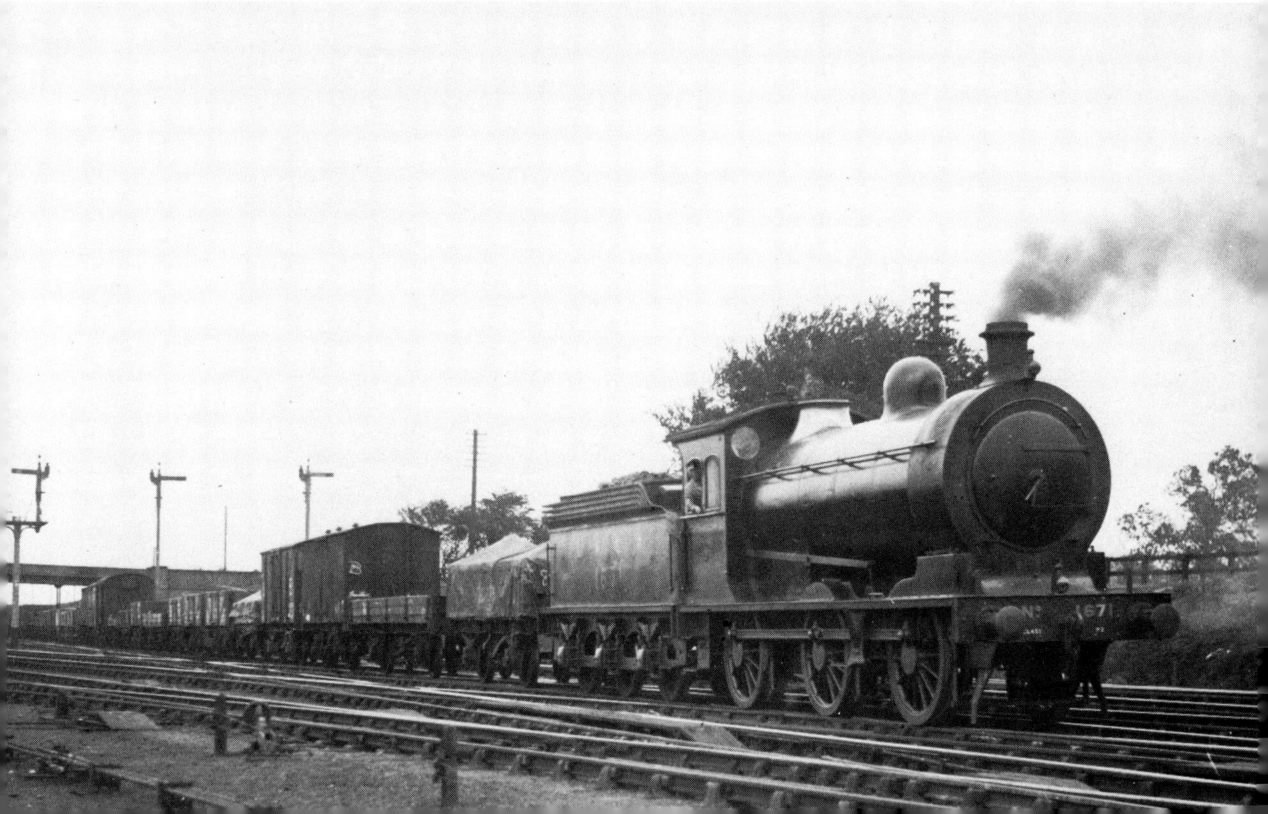

Top: Class J27 (NER Class P3) 0-6-0 No. 2392 on an up goods near Hett Mill in May 1926. This engine is now working on the North Yorkshire Moors Railway.

Above: Class J39 0-6-0 No. 1450 on an up goods at Alne, 16 July 1927. The coach in the right background was owned by the Easingwold Railway./*H. G. W. Household*

Top: Class B15 (NER Class S2) 4-6-0 No. 798 passing Croft Spa on an up express./*W. Rogerson*

Above: Class B16 4-6-0 No. 923 on an up braked goods at Chester Moor Colliery, 2 June 1926./*H. G. W. Household*

Top: Class Q7 (NER T3) 0-8-0 No. 633 passing Usworth, on the 'old main line' on 28 August 1926./*H. G. W. Household*

Above: Class A1 4-6-2 No. 2576 *The White Knight* leaving York on a down express. 7 May 1927./*H. G. W. Household*

22

Top: Class C8 (NER Class 4CC) 4-4-2 No. 731 passing Portobello on an up express, with GWR coaches leading./*T. G. Hepburn*

Above: Class D11 4-4-0 *Gerard Powys Dewhurst* on the down 'Harrogate Pullman' south of Tadcaster./*S. Ellingworth*

Top: Class A1 4-6-2 No. 4475 *Flying Fox* on the inaugural run of 9.50am Kings Cross-Newcastle non-stop on 11 July 1927, passing York./*H. G. W. Household*

Above: Class Q6 (NER T2) 0-8-0 on goods at Croft Spa, 4 June 1927./*W. Rogerson*

1930-1934

A further eight Gresley A3 Pacifics appeared in 1930. Gateshead received Nos 2595-9, whilst Nos 2795/6/7 went to Haymarket. Two of the latter, Nos 2795 *Call Boy* and 2796 *Spearmint,* received corridor tenders and soon became favourites for the non-stop 'Flying Scotsman' from the Edinburgh end. In fact it was No 2795 that worked the first up non-stop in 1932 (with No 4472 *Flying Scotsman* on the down train) in the accelerated timings introduced in that year.

The long-overdue speeding up of East Coast trains actually began on 1 May 1932 when the 'Flying Scotsman', on its winter schedule, was booked into Edinburgh 25 minutes earlier at 5.50pm as against the long-established 6.15pm (public time). With the summer timetable, which came into force on 18 July 1932, the non-stop timing was cut to 7½ hours and the train arrived in Edinburgh at 5.30pm, and when the winter timetable was resumed in September another five minutes were shaved off to get the train into Edinburgh at 5.45pm.

Also from 1 May 1932 the 'Queen of Scots' Pullman was accelerated by 20 minutes between London and Edinburgh, bringing the time down to eight hours, and other trains received the same treatment. On the same date the engines and men on the 10.0am, 1.20pm, and 5.30pm expresses from Kings Cross commenced working through to Newcastle, returning the following day; the rosters were covered alternately by Kings Cross and Gateshead locomotives and crews. In fact 1 May 1932 could be said to be the start of the most momentous period in the history of the East Coast main line, which in the next seven years saw the introduction of high-speed trains and notable locomotive developments.

After years of discussion and design the Gresley-Yarrow high-pressure locomotive No 10000 was turned out from Darlington Works in December 1929, although it was not actually handed over to the Running Department until 20 June 1930. The water-tube boiler was constructed at Messrs Yarrow's works at Scotstoun, Glasgow, and the frame and wheels were sent from Darlington to Scotstoun in April 1929 for the boiler to be fitted. Six months later the almost completed locomotive was despatched from Scotstoun to Darlington Works, with strict in-

structions that "when the engine leaves Messrs Yarrow's yard this engine must be sheeted up before the LMS inspect the engine for gauge". It must be remembered that at this time the LMS also had under construction a high-pressure locomotive (No 6399 *Fury*) and obviously the LNER did not want the LMS to know what the engine was like. In fact, the secrecy in which the LNER engine was built led to its christening as the 'Hush-Hush' – a name that stuck for a long time. No 10000 was never officially named, although at one time there was a scheme under consideration to call it *British Enterprise.*

A feature which intrigued the press and the public of the period was that when viewed from the side the engine appeared to have no chimney. It had one, of course, but to assist smoke and steam clearance the chimney was placed low down between two deflector plates and thus could be seen only from the front. The shape and form of the deflector plates were settled early on in the design stage, but with a normal cylindrical smokebox. This left very little room for a chimney, so the smokebox was re-arranged with a sloping top, after Gresley had written to R. J. Robson, the Chief Draughtsman at Darlington, to say that he did not care for the design of the blast pipe or chimney. Robson prepared new drawings for the front end after a rough sketch of the proposals had been approved by Gresley and the smokebox was modified at Yarrow's, although Darlington supplied a new front plate with smokebox door to fit the new arrangement. The corridor tender was built at Doncaster and worked to Darlington in November 1929 at the same time as the engine was being hauled in stages from Scotstoun to Darlington.

The engine was rapidly completed at Darlington. Official photographs of the locomotive were taken in the Paint Shop yard, and issued on 10 December 1929: two days later No 10000 made its first trial run. By the end of December it was working test trains between Darlington and Newcastle, but it is not clear if these were normal passenger trains or simply comprised empty coaching stock. The engine was painted grey and remained in this livery for the whole of its life in its original form; later, after rebuilding at Doncaster in 1937, it was painted the standard garter blue of the LNER streamlined locomotives.

The real flurry of publicity came in January 1930. No 10000 was worked up to Kings Cross on the 7th, and on the 8th there was a press view of the engine, so that the following morning views of the 'hush-hush' engine appeared in many of the national morning papers, introducing its unusual outline to countless readers. Trial trips continued to be worked: for instance, on 6 February 1930 No 10000 ran from Darlington to Doncaster and back with 400tons, and on 13 February from Darlington to Kings Cross with 500tons, returning the following day. On the latter runs timings were generous – 5hr 7min to reach Kings Cross, with stops totalling 16min at Doncaster and Grantham, and 5hr 12min on the return, with stops totalling 33min. Darlington depart to York pass was allowed 54 min on the up journey, and the same for York pass to Darlington arrive on the return.

On 22 February 1930 No 10000, with the dynamometer car, was worked to Edinburgh for trials in Scotland, although the main object of this run seems to have been to photograph the engine and train on the Forth Bridge for publicity purposes.

After being handed over for traffic in June 1930 the engine was allocated to Gateshead shed and used on normal passenger services, one of the most important being the up 'Queen of Scots' between Newcastle and Leeds, leaving Newcastle at 1.57pm and arriving at Leeds (Central) at 4.10pm. This the engine worked on its very first day, 21 June 1930, and on numerous other occasions. It was also used on the 11.17am Newcastle to Edinburgh (8.55am Leeds-Glasgow) and the 5.12pm Edinburgh-York (4.0pm Glasgow-Leeds), returning from York to Tyneside on an express goods. Another favourite working was the 12.23pm Newcastle to Edinburgh (10.5am York-Perth), returning from Edinburgh on the up Aberdeen fish train at 5.27pm, although on this working No 10000 was usually replaced at Newcastle instead of completing the second leg of the diagram to York and back. The most notable working, however, was on 31 July 1930 when No 10000 headed the up non-stop 'Flying Scotsman' from Edinburgh to London, returning the following day on the down train.

No 10000 was fitted with a turbo-generator under the cab and this supplied electricity for the lights in the cab and the headlights. These were normal locomotive oil lamps converted to electricity and they plugged into a socket adjacent to each lamp bracket so that the correct headcode could be displayed day or night.

The greatest difficulty appears to have been encountered in making the engine steam well and various combinations of baffles were fitted between the water tubes to improve matters. The reducing valves for the auxiliaries also gave trouble and had to be replaced, and in August 1933 the telemotor reversing equipment was replaced by hand screw gear. Another modification was

carried out when in September 1930 Gresley ordered liners $1\frac{5}{8}$in thick to be put in the two high-pressure cylinders in place of the $\frac{5}{8}$in liners, thus reducing the cylinder diameter from 12in to 10in In July 1932 there was a scheme to restore the cylinders to 12in and the original piston heads and rods were located at Darlington Works, but they were not used. An odd feature of No 10000 was that the front spectacles were of unequal size.

The advent of new D49 4-4-0 engines ('Hunts') in 1932 meant a reshuffle of the five NE Area oscillating cam engines and they were transferred to Hull to work Sheffield trains – Nos 318/20/2 from Neville Hill and Nos 327 and 335 from York. This meant that Leeds now used the new engines Nos 201 *The Bramham Moor*, 211 *The York and Ainsty*, and 220 *The Zetland* on their Newcastle turns. York received Nos 232/5/47/55/69/83/8/97/8 in 1932 and 1933, but after a few weeks Nos 283 and 297 were transferred to Heaton. Previously Newcastle had seen only the D49 engines from York and Leeds in the south, or Edinburgh in the north, as none of the class had previously been stationed on Tyneside.

A number of the 1934 batch went to Gateshead and these, together with Nos 201, 211 and 220 displaced from Leeds by others of the 1934 series, worked in the area, mainly on the Carlisle line rather than the main line, although for a time they were to be seen on the 9.32am Newcastle-Edinburgh (the 8.35am ex Darlington) and the return working at 2.30pm. However, the York and Leeds engines continued to work on the main line but not normally on the top East Coast trains. One of the Heaton engines was tried on the Pullman working from Newcastle to Harrogate and Leeds (Central).

The two C7 Atlantics rebuilt in 1931 with a booster bogie forming an articulated unit between engine and tender, Nos 727 and 2171, were both York engines and as the main purpose of the rebuilding was to provide extra power on Cockburnspath bank they were both transferred to Gateshead on 3 December 1931 in exchange for Nos 719 and 737, also C7 engines. However, although successful on trial the two rebuilds (reclassified C9) did not perform well in actual service; they were often to be found as assistant engines, since they could not safely be let out on their own! They spent a lot of time out of service and they were not popular, partly because of the steam that came up through the floorboards of the cab when the booster was in operation. The boosters were removed in 1936/7 and the engines continued to run as articulated locomotives, but they were not a great success and went to the scrapheap in April 1942 (No 2171) and January 1943 (No 727), being the first of the North Eastern three-cylinder Atlantics to go.

Two further Atlantics which fell from grace were Nos 730 and 731, the Smith compound engines, which had performed so well on the main line from their introduction in 1906. They worked regularly on the main line until about 1930 when, with the influx of new engines, they became redundant: they subsequently spent a short time at Hull for trials on the Sheffield trains, but they were soon returned to Gateshead. In November 1933 the Locomotive Running Superintendent issued an instruction that they were 'to be transferred from Gateshead to Heaton, put in good order and placed in stock and utilised at busy holiday periods'. However, when No 731 entered Darlington Works in the following month it was decided that it should be withdrawn from traffic, leaving No 730 to run until January 1935, when it too was withdrawn, after running approximately 750,000 miles. During 1933 No 730 spent some time at exhibitions of rolling stock for school children.

In 1930 Tweedmouth lost its allocation of C6 Atlantics and the 20 engines of the class were divided between Gateshead (Nos 295, 696/9, 700/4, 1753/94), Heaton (Nos 649, 742/84, 1776), York (Nos 532, 698, 701, 1680, 1792) and Darlington (Nos 697, 702/3/5). The Darlington engines were used mainly as main-line stand -by pilots and had little regular work allocated to them; the others of the class were used on secondary main-line duties and as pilots on heavier than usual trains, double-heading a Pacific, or perhaps with a C7.

Although by the mid-1930s Gateshead and Heaton had 25 Pacifics between them York had none and their main-line workings had to be handled by D49 4-4-0 and C7 4-4-2 engines – not that York had any really important jobs as these were performed by the Kings Cross, Grantham, Gateshead, Heaton and Haymarket engines, However, early in 1934 York shed required a powerful engine to work the 8.12pm to Newcastle (4.0pm ex Kings Cross), which stopped at Thirsk, Northallerton, Darlington and Durham, and on 9 February 1934 No 2401 *City of Kingston upon Hull* was transferred from Gateshead to York in exchange for C7 No 716; No 2403 *City of Durham* followed on 26 April and 2400 *City of Newcastle* on 7 May (in exchange for C7 No 2167). With the advent of more new Gresley Pacifics in 1934, Nos 2501 *Colombo*, 2503 *Firdaussi* and 2507 *Singapore* were allocated to Gateshead and these released No 2402 *City of York* to York on 13 August 1934, followed by No 2404 *City of Ripon* on 7 November

1934. These Raven Pacifics were used mainly on York's Newcastle turns, although they did work up to Kings Cross, one regular working being on the 12.16pm up from York on Fridays, returning on the down 'Norseman' on summer Saturdays.

At Gateshead the shed buildings were mainly roundhouses with turntables of insufficient size to accommodate the Pacific engines, but for these it was possible to use a straight shed converted from the tender shop of Gateshead Works. For turning the engines there were the Gateshead and King Edward Bridge triangles conveniently located at each end of the shed. At Heaton the depot consisted of a straight shed and so the engines could be housed under cover without much trouble, but there was no convenient triangle on which to turn the engines, so a 70ft turntable was installed early in 1925. At York Pacific engines were turned on a triangle formed by the goods lines, until a 70ft turntable was installed in 1932. However, this was in the shed yard and as the building consisted of four roundhouses it was impossible to stand the Raven Pacific engines under cover – hence photographs of the class at York, usually taken at a week-end on RCTS or SLS shed visits, show them standing outside in the yard. If repairs were required, perhaps needing the use of the wheel drops inside the shed, the tender had to be uncoupled from the engine before it could be manoeuvred on to a turntable and then off into an appropriate stall or road.

Soon after their arrival at York the Raven Pacifics were fitted with Gresley eight-wheel tenders in an attempt to improve their sphere of operations, but this modification did not prolong their life. In fact, some were withdrawn for scrapping less than two years after the fitting of the eight-wheel tenders. The new tenders were not scrapped with the engines but reconditioned for use behind Gresley Pacifics. The final three Raven Pacifics were actually built by the LNER in 1924 and when scrapped in 1936/7 they were the first LNER-built engines to be withdrawn.

In the 1930s Sir W. G. Armstrong Whitworth & Co of Newcastle were developing the diesel locomotive and railcar side of their business. The railcars were diesel-electric and the LNER tried, and eventually purchased, four – three 250hp cars and one 95hp. The three larger cars were put into service with the names *Tyneside Venturer, Lady Hamilton* and *Northumbrian*, but the small car remained un-named.

The Armstrong Whitworth locomotives of the period ranged in size from small yard shunters to large mobile power houses for Brazil and into this range came the 72tons 880hp diesel-electric locomotive built at Scotswood in 1933. A demonstration run was made on 6 July 1933 from Newcastle to North Wylam and back, with seven coaches, and from 7 February 1934 the engine was worked by the LNER on goods trains between Newcastle and Berwick, and York. The trials were scheduled to last for four months under normal railway operating conditions and it was agreed that the locomotive would be manned by railway company's footplate crews accompanied by a skilled mechanic from the makers.

The first main-line passenger working with this engine took place on 7 June 1934, when it headed a train of eight tourist coaches conveying an Institute of Transport party from Leeds to the LNER permanent way Reclamation Depot at Darlington. The train left Leeds at 1.25pm, running via Harrogate and Thirsk and arriving at Darlington at 3.24pm: there was a 41min stop at Thirsk. On the return journey Darlington was left at 5.3pm and this time the train travelled via Sinderby to Harrogate and Leeds, where it was due at 6.22pm. At Darlington the complete train was turned on the triangle at Geneva. To work the special the engine was sent light from Heaton shed to Neville Hill on the previous day; it was manned by a Heaton crew who were normally in charge of it.

The locomotive was of the 1-Co-1 wheel arrangement, with an assymetrical body because of the mounting at one end of an auxiliary engine and generator set. The engine was an eight-cylinder Armstrong-Sulzer diesel consuming 1.3 gallons of oil per mile when working heavy trains. At last the diesel-electric main line locomotive had arrived in this country, but it was to be another 24 years before such engines could be seen in regular service on the East Coast main line.

The little North Sunderland Railway, which ran between Chathill and Seahouses (on the Northumberland coast), used a small 85hp Armstrong-Whitworth diesel-electric locomotive from 1934. This, named *The Lady Armstrong*, could be seen standing at the head of the branch train in the bay platform at the north end (up side) of Chathill LNER station.

In the early 1930s the Kitson-Still diesel-steam locomotive was at work in the York area. It had originally been built by Kitson & Co of Leeds in 1927 (Works No 5374), with eight cylinders in two groups of four arranged horizontally across the locomotive. One group of cylinders was placed below the front end of the boiler, and the other in front of the cab, all driving on to a common crankshaft placed across the engine. The locomotive had an oil-fired boiler supplying steam at 180lb sq in to the inner end of each cylinder and

this power was used to start the locomotive from rest and accelerate it to about 6mph. Around this speed the outer ends of the same cylinders started to operate on the compression ignition principle and the steam supply was gradually shut down until the engine was running on diesel power only. The exhaust from the diesel cycle was used to heat the boiler water so that when necessary – to climb steep banks, etc – the burner could be turned on and steam generated quickly to be used in the cylinders to assist the diesel working. Although built in 1927 it was not until 1932/3 that the locomotive was placed in regular service on goods trains working from York.

On the freight side there was a reshuffle of J27 0-6-0 engines because it was desired to have engines with balanced wheels at specific sheds for certain duties. Thus Nos 2352/3 moved from West Hartlepool to York, and Nos 2386/92 from Ferryhill to York in February 1930 for use on Newcastle goods turns.

In the 1930s new K3 2-6-0s were taking over many of the fast goods turns but some sheds—York in particular—used them extensively on secondary passenger and excursion workings. Tweedmouth and Heaton received a number of new K3s for the North Main Line (Newcastle-Berwick-Edinburgh) workings, displacing B16 4-6-0s to Hull: in fact Dairycoates, which had no B16s on 1 January 1925, received 26 over the next decade, and by the end of 1934 Heaton had 16 K3s and Tweedmouth 13.

At this period the braked fish trains from the North were frequently given an assistant engine between Edinburgh and Newcastle. North British classes noted on such duties included D29, D30, D31, D33 and D34 4-4-0s, as well as some of the Scottish 'Director' and 'Shire' 4-4-0s.

Between Alne and Green Lane (Thirsk) the main line was equipped with Hall's automatic semaphore signals controlled by track circuits. The signals themselves were operated by gas under pressure and the valves governing the gas and thus the position of the arms, were activated by electrical currents dependent upon the track circuits. Approach-lighted colour-light signals were introduced on the main line between Eryholme and Black Banks (south of Darlington) on 12 February 1928, but the first major installation was carried out with the widening of the main line between Alne and Pilmoor in the early 1930s. Under this scheme it was decided to replace the automatic semaphore signals (which had seen almost 30 years' faithful service) with automatic electric colour-light signals, and to extend the new installation to Poppleton Junction in the south and

Northallerton in the north, with new boxes at Beningbrough, Alne, Sessay Wood (later Pilmoor South and eventually Pilmoor), Thirsk and Otterington. Further extensions northwards brought in new electric boxes at Northallerton, Eryholme, and Darlington South in 1939, together with the modernisation of the Eryholme-Black Banks installation of 1928.

After teething troubles way back in 1905 the automatic semaphore signals worked well and the system was trusted by the drivers. However, trouble did occur, such as the time when a signalman noticed that a petrol inspection car and a freight train were running under the same clear signals! The automatic signals normally stood in the clear position and as the petrol car was not operating the track circuits the signals were not going to danger behind it. This was overcome by fitting the cars with metal brushes bearing on the head of the rails.

Raven's mechanical fog signalling apparatus was also fitted on the main line and in LNER days only engines with the equipment were allowed to work trains over the York-Alnmouth section. Even light engines going to Works, if not fitted with the apparatus, had to put into the nearest engine shed if they encountered fog or falling snow.

The introduction of the colour-light signals brought a different hazard under the 'One Minute (Stop and Proceed) Rule', whereby drivers were allowed to pass certain signals at danger after waiting for one minute. Over-confidence, mis-judgement of speed, and the brightness of the signals, led to a number of rear-end collisions where the driver of the second train was unable to stop in time after sighting the tail-lamp of the first train.

The most serious accident occurred on the evening of 6 December 1933 near Alne, not long after the signals had been installed, when the 6.53pm fish train from Newcastle (C7 engine No 2209) ran into the back of the 5.55pm express goods from Newcastle (B16 engine No 932). The second train had moved forward from an automatic signal after waiting for one minute, when it collided with the train in front which was just moving off from a controlled colour-light signal. The ensuing wreckage fouled the down main line and this was run into by C7 No 2196 on the 8.12pm York-Newcastle. Fortunately the only injury was to the dining car conductor on the passenger train, who sustained a bruised hand. All three tracks were blocked for 20 hours, when the down slow was opened, but the two main lines remained closed for a further seven hours.

The Stop and Proceed rule was not new on this section as it had also applied to the automatic semaphore signals, but drivers were misled by seeing green lights ahead which actually referred to a train in front of them.

Two similar incidents involving goods trains occurred at Poppleton Junction in August and September 1933, and another, this time involving passenger trains – on 6 August 1934, when the 10.45pm Newcastle-Kings Cross (Engine No 2575 *Galopin*) ran into the rear of the 7.45pm Edinburgh-Kings Cross (engine No 2574 *St. Frusquin*).

The trouble was overcome by fitting telephones at all automatic and semi-automatic signals (those which worked automatically or, when required, could be controlled by a signalman) and allowing a train to pass a signal at danger only on a signalman's instructions. Thus the driver could be advised of the position ahead of him. Only in special cases could a driver pass a colour-light signal at danger without first receiving permission from a signalman.

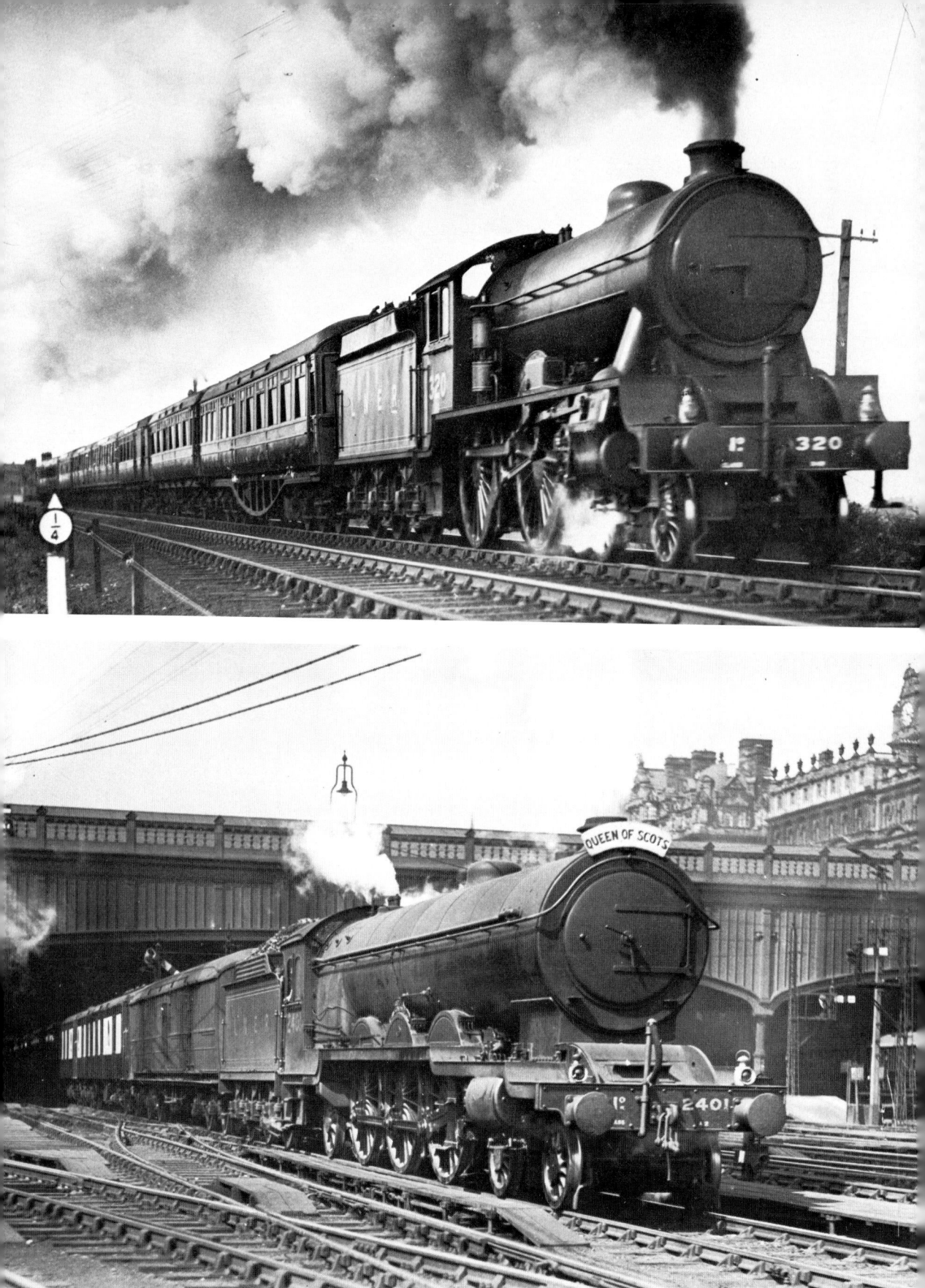

Above left: Class D49 4-4-0 No. 320 *Warwickshire* near Seaton Carew on a Newcastle-Liverpool train. The two leading vehicles — a 12-wheel restaurant car and a first open — will be detached at Leeds./*W. L. Good*

Above: Class A2 No. 2404, fitted with Gresley boiler, leaving York./*W. H. Whitworth*

Left: Class A2 4-6-2 No. 2401 *City of Kingston upon Hull* leaving Edinburgh (Waverley) with the up 'Queen of Scots' Pullman train./*T. G. Hepburn*

Below: Haymarket shed with (l. to r.) Class A3 4-6-2s Nos. 2596 *Manna,* 2573 *Harvester,* Class A1 No. 2563 *William Whitelaw,* and Class A2 No. 2402 *City of York.*/*W. H. Whitworth*

Top: Class C7 4-4-2 No. 2196 at Ripon with the up 'Queen of Scots.'/*J. G. Pearson*

Above: The four varieties of NER Atlantics in York shed on 28 August 1932: (l. to r.) C7 No. 2208, C8 No. 730, C6 No. 532, and C6 (V/09) No. 703./*H. C. Casserley*

Top: Class A1 No. 2582 *Sir Hugo* on the down 'Queen of Scots' at Headingley./*S. Ellingworth*

Above: Class J21 0-6-0 No. 34 leaving Darlington on the tool vans and steam crane 28 May 1932./*W. Rogerson*

Top: Class W1 4-6-4 No. 10000 entering Darlington (Bank Top) station on an up express on 26 June 1930. Although six months old the engine had been handed over to the Running Department only six days earlier./*W. Rogerson*

Above: Class D49/3 4-4-0 No. 318 Cambridgeshire at York – one of the six engines built with oscillating cam gear./*Real Photos Ltd*

Top: Class A2 4-6-2 No. 2400 *City of Newcastle* approaching Edinburgh Waverley on an empty stock train to form a working to the south, on 1 August 1931./*H. C. Casserley*

Above: Class A3 4-6-2 No. 2580 *Shotover* passing Croft Spa during the first week of non-stop working between London and Edinburgh, on 5 May 1928./*W. Rogerson*

Above: Class C7 4-4-2 No. 2198 passing Northallerton on an up express./*H. G. Tidey*

Below: Class A1 4-6-2 No. 2546 *Donovan* at York./*W. L. Good*

Above: Class B13 4-6-0 No. 761 on an up goods climbing Dalton Bank, south of Darlington, on 7 June 1930./*W. Rogerson*

Below: Class B15 4-6-0 No. 797 passing Ferryhill on a goods. /*W. L. Good*

Top: The pioneer North Eastern Atlantic, No. 532, passing Cowton on 5 June 1933./*W. Rogerson*

Above: Two Great Northern Atlantics leaving York on an up express./*H. G. Tidey*

Top: Class K3 2-6-0 No. 1394 passing Ferryhill./*W. L. Good*

*Above:*Class A3 4-6-2 No. 2599 *Book Law* passing Manors on the approach to Newcastle from the north./*Author's Collection*

1935-1939

The period under review was pre-dated by an event which took place outside the North Eastern Area but which merits mention because of its effect on main line train services. I refer to the test runs of No 4472 *Flying Scotsman* from Kings Cross to Leeds and back on 30 November 1934. On this occasion the 185.8 miles from Kings Cross to Leeds (Central) were covered in 151 min. 56 sec.: the load comprised four vehicles, one of which was the former North Eastern dynamometer car. The test run was reputed to be for comparison with the running then being performed by high-speed railcar sets in Germany, and it proved that similar performances could be achieved by a steam locomotive if required.

Following the lessons learned on the above test run it was decided to carry out a similar trial run between London and Newcastle. It is obvious that by 5 March 1935, when the Newcastle run took place, thoughts in the LNER hierarchy were already turned towards a high-speed London-Newcastle service, although in his Annual Report issued on 1 March Mr. William Whitelaw, Chairman of the company, did not commit himself, saying that further trials were necessary.

On the test run to Newcastle A3 Pacific No 2750 *Papyrus* was provided, worked in the down direction by Driver H. Gutteridge and Fireman A. Wightman, and in the up by Driver W. Sparshatt and Fireman R. Webster, all of Kings Cross shed. The latter pair had been the crew on No 4472 on the Leeds test run in the previous November.

The train left Kings Cross at 9.8am and the schedule allowed exactly four hours for the 268.3 miles to Newcastle, passing Shaftholme Junction, 160.2 miles, in 137 minutes, leaving 103 minutes to cover the remaining 108.1 miles to Newcastle. Due to a derailment just north of Doncaster Shaftholme was passed 4 min 1 sec late, but even so the arrival time at Newcastle was 2 min 53 sec early, so that an improvement of almost seven minutes was made on the booked timing.

Returning south, at 3.47pm from Newcastle, Shaftholme Junction was passed in 99 min 3 sec, almost four minutes under schedule, with speed well in the eighties for most of the way between Darlington and York. Kings Cross was reached in 231 min 48 sec – a slight improvement on the down journey. The North Eastern Area was represented

on the train by A. Collinson, Acting Superintendent; C. M. Stedman, Locomotive Running Superintendent; and J. J. Lovatt, Assistant Locomotive Running Superintendent.

Three days later, on 8 March 1935, at the Company's Annual General Meeting Mr. Whitelaw announced that in the autumn it was hoped to introduce a high-speed train between London and Newcastle, to be called 'The Silver Jubilee' – and this only seven days after he had refused to confirm that such a train was planned. Clearly the exploits of 'Papyrus', Sparshatt and Gutteridge, had proved that there was still some life in the steam locomotive!

The advent of the A4 streamlined Pacifics has often been told, notably in the RCTS publication *Locomotives of the LNER* Part 2A. First thoughts on a streamlined Pacific early in 1934 produced an outline similar to that of the P1 2-8-2 *Cock o' the North* in its original form, but this design was modified a number of times and, in fact, changes in the streamlined casing were still being made when the first of the class, No 2509 *Silver Link*, was under construction. The engine was completed in September 1935 and sent to Kings Cross shed on the 13th which, as it turned out, proved to be a good omen and not a bad one! On 27 September it headed a demonstration special from Kings Cross to Barkston and back, in preparation for the inaugural run of the new train on 1 October.

The North Eastern Area played only a very small part in the actual running of the 'Silver Jubilee' train. The engine was stationed at Kings Cross and worked by Kings Cross crews, who lodged at Gateshead overnight whilst their engine was prepared for the up train the following day. The timings were:

Newcastle (dep.) 10.0am
Darlington (arr.) 10.40am
　　　　　(dep.) 10.42am
York (pass 11.19am (11.23am)
Shaftholme Junc. (pass) 11.45am (11.48½am)
Kings Cross (arr.) 2.0pm

Kings Cross (dep.) 5.30pm
Shaftholme Junc. (pass) 7.45 (7.42½pm)
York (pass) 8.9pm (8.6½pm)
Darlington (arr.) 8.48pm
　　　　　(dep.) 8.50pm
Newcastle (arr.) 9.30pm

It was found that the colour-light signalling north of York was not suited to the high-speed running of the train and until adjustments could be made the timing was amended so that four minutes extra were allowed between Darlington and York in the up direction and $2\frac{1}{2}$ minutes in the down as indicated in the brackets. The original accommodation, seating 78 first-class and 120 third-class passengers, consisted of seven coaches but the train's popularity necessitated extra seating and in 1938 this was achieved by converting a twin articulated coach into a triplet. A supplementary charge of 5s first class and 3s third class was made for each single journey.

It was not until the third engine, No 2511 *Silver King*, was built that one of the streamlined engines was allocated to Gateshead shed. After standing by as the emergency engine, in case of failure of the Kings Cross engine on the 10.0am up 'Silver Jubilee', *Silver King* worked the 11.10am Newcastle-Edinburgh (9.0am Leeds-Glasgow), returning on the up working of the same train (later named 'The North Briton') at 5.10pm from Waverley (4.0pm from Glasgow). It was this engine which was chosen to make a test run from Newcastle to Edinburgh and back on Saturday 26 September 1936, using the 'Silver Jubilee' set, in readiness for the proposed high-speed 'Coronation' train between London, Edinburgh, and Aberdeen.

Possibilities south of Newcastle were already known after a year's experience with the 'Silver Jubilee', but north of Newcastle no greatly accelerated timings had been attempted. The test train was worked by Driver T. Dron of Gateshead and the 124 miles between Newcastle and Edinburgh were covered in 118 minutes in the down direction and 114 in the up – 30 minutes faster than the contemporary 'Flying Scotsman'. Thus the way was clear for a six-hour schedule between London and Edinburgh, with stops at York in the down direction and Newcastle in the up: extension of the train north of Edinburgh was abandoned. The timings between Edinburgh and Shaftholme Junction were:

Kings Cross (arr.)	–	10.30pm
(dep.)	4.0pm	–
Shaftholme Junction (pass)	6.12½pm	8.18½pm
York (arr.)	6.37pm	–
(pass)	–	7.53pm
(dep.)	6.40pm	–
Darlington (pass)	7.21pm	7.13pm
Newcastle (dep.)	–	6.33pm
(pass)	8.0pm	–
(arr.)	–	6.30pm
Berwick (pass)	9.5pm	5.25pm
Edinburgh (arr.)	10.0pm	–
(dep.)	–	4.30pm

The down train, with its 157min booking for the 188.2 miles to York, was timed at an average speed of 71.9mph – the highest worked in this country up to that time. North of York the average was 61.4mph.

Again crews from the three Areas were used – Southern (Kings Cross); North Eastern (Gateshead); and Scottish (Haymarket), using A4 engines from Kings Cross and Haymarket. The absence of a Newcastle stop in the down direction meant that on Mondays, Wednesdays and Fridays a set of Gateshead men had to travel as passengers to York on the 4.14pm train (York arr. 5.52pm) and then take over the down 'Coronation' from another set of Gateshead men, which they worked through to Edinburgh. They then returned home the following day working the up 'Coronation' as far as Newcastle on Tuesdays and Thursdays and the 2.30pm Edinburgh-Newcastle on Saturdays. The opposite set of Gateshead men worked the 5.20pm up to London on Sundays and the up 'Coronation' on Tuesdays and Thursdays, returning the following days (Mondays, Wednesdays and Fridays) on the down 'Coronation' at 4.0pm from Kings Cross, being relieved at York by the set of men mentioned above, and returning home as passengers on the 6.45pm slow to Darlington, where they had to change on to the 5.0pm Liverpool-Newcastle, which got them into Newcastle at 9.13pm.

The Haymarket men worked the up 'Coronation' to Newcastle on Mondays, Wednesdays and Fridays, and after being relieved by Kings Cross men travelled forward to York on Mondays and Wednesdays as passengers on the 7.10pm from Newcastle (the Bristol mail) in order to lodge at York. The following day (Tuesdays and Thursdays) they worked the 'Coronation' from York to Edinburgh. On Fridays they lodged on Tyneside and returned home on the Saturday working the 9.32am semi-fast.

Kings Cross men worked down to Newcastle on the 6.0pm on Sundays, and the 4.0pm 'Coronation' as far as York on Tuesdays and Thursdays. They then continued to Newcastle on the 6.45pm Darlington slow to lodge at Newcastle, returning on the up 'Coronation' on Mondays, Wednesdays, and Fridays.

The first down train on Monday 5 July 1937 was worked throughout by No 4491 *Commonwealth of Australia* with Driver T. Dron and Fireman C. R. Charlton, relieved at York by Driver H. Hutchinson and Fireman S. Jobling, also of Gateshead. In the up direction the engine was No 4489 *Dominion of Canada* in the hands of Driver J. Binnie and Fireman M. Brand of Haymarket as far as Newcastle, and Driver G. Burfoot and Fireman W. Middleton of Kings Cross forward to London. Driver Burfoot had been on the press and demonstration run from Kings Cross to Barkston and back on Wednesday 30 June, and Driver Binnie was in charge of the engine on a similar run from Edinburgh to Newcastle and back on Friday 2 July.

With the introducton of a Newcastle stop for the down train from 7 March 1938 it was possible to simplify the men's workings. Haymarket men daily worked the up 'Coronation' between Edinburgh and Newcastle, returning on the down 'Coronation', whilst south of Newcastle Kings Cross and Gateshead men worked alternately, Gateshead men taking the down train from Kings Cross to Newcastle on Mondays, Wednesdays, and Fridays, and the up train from Newcastle to Kings Cross on Tuesdays and Thursdays. Kings Cross men had the down train on Tuesdays and Thursdays, and the up on Mondays, Wednesdays and Fridays.

I was at York on the fine evening of Monday, 5 June 1937, when a very large crowd assembled expectantly at the north end of No 5 platform (now No 9) to watch the arrival and departure of the first down 'Coronation'. This arrived 1½min early with 4491 and departed on time after changing the Gateshead crews; however, very few stayed on to watch the up train go through non-stop 75min later behind No 4489.

Over the next two years I frequently saw the up and down 'Coronation' trains and the down 'Silver Jubilee', particularly during the long evenings in May to August. I regularly used to visit the main line near Sessay to see these trains streaking effortlessly along the Plain of York and a vantage point on a minor road which went under the main line enabled me to have a panoramic view of the trains running on this famous stretch. The most impressive spectacle was to see them at dusk, with the headlamps twinkling in the distance, a 'swoosh' as the train passed, and a short glimpse of comfortable coach interiors, with the passengers relaxing as they travelled at 70mph or more. The streamlined trains were withdrawn on the outbreak of World War II.

The A4s on the streamlined trains did have their troubles at times, but the locomotives were given special attention and performed lengthy spells on the high-speed trains; some of them ran without a break for four or five weeks, used indiscriminately on the 'Silver Jubilee,' 'Coronation', 'West Riding Limited', or 'Flying Scotsman'. One problem was the inability of the engine on the up 'Coronation' to reach Kings Cross with the coal available in the tender, particularly during the winter months, and on occasions a pilot had to be taken at Hitchin for the last 32 miles. This was soon overcome by more careful coaling at Haymarket shed.

Engine failures did occur, however, and at times A1, A3 and V2 engines could be seen on the streamlined trains. On the occasion of an engine failure en route the nearest locomotive was pressed into use. On one occasion (14 April 1937) A4 No 2512 failed at Browney, south of Durham, and G5 0-4T No 1752 hauled the 'Silver Jubilee' on to Newcastle. On another memorable occasion A4 No 4482 failed at Grantham, where No 10000 was provided as a replacement. This in turn failed at Durham and again a G5 came to the rescue in the shape of No 1837, to take the train on to Newcastle. For the final stage of the journey No 2575 *Galopin* was used, but even so the 'Coronation' arrived at Edinburgh 57 minutes late.

The various colour schemes adopted for the A4 streamlined engines cause some confusion. The first four, Nos 2509-12, built in 1935, were painted silver grey to haul the 'Silver Jubilee' train. These were followed in 1936/7 by a series of similar engines (Nos 4482-7) painted standard LNER green for working normal expresses. The forthcoming 'Coronation' express led to a trial of various shades of blue on No 4488 *Osprey* in April and May 1937, whilst No 4489 *Woodcock* was turned out temporarily in a grey livery. When garter blue had been decided upon for the 'Coronation' engines these two, together with Nos 4490, 4491 and 4492, were painted in the new livery and all were named after Dominion or Commonwealth countries.

The next three engines (Nos 4493, 4494 and 4495) were turned out in the green livery, but Nos 4495 was repainted blue, and together with 4496, specially prepared to work the 'West Riding Limited' streamlined train between London and Leeds. By this time it was becoming obvious that silver engines could not always be rostered for the 'Silver Jubilee', nor blue engines for the 'Coronation' and 'West Riding Limited', and all subsequent engines were turned out in the garter blue livery, with dark red wheels. The four silver engines and the eight green engines were repainted blue as they passed through Doncaster Works, a task which was completed in September 1938 when No 4494 was repainted. No 10000, the erstwhile 'hush-hush' engine, was also in blue livery when it emerged from Doncaster Works in its rebuilt form in October 1937.

The introduction of the third high-speed train on the main line, the 'West Riding Limited' between London and Leeds, on 27 September

1937 brought about a change of route for the up 'Yorkshire Pullman'. From Harrogate the train commenced to work via York, leaving Harrogate at 11.15am, passing Knaresborough at 11.21½am, to give an arrival time at York of 11.40am. After a five-minute stop York was left at 11.45am and Shaftholme passed at 12.15pm, reaching Doncaster six minutes later. Four minutes were allowed to change the engine and attach the Hull and Halifax cars before the train left for Kings Cross.

For this duty Starbeck acquired the rebuilt D20, No 2020, from York in exchange for No 1232, and No 2020 made a fine sight striding along the main line at the head of four spotless Pullman cars. The engine and men returned on the 5.5pm Doncaster-Harrogate (1.40pm ex Kings Cross) via Knottingley, Church Fenton and Wetherby, due in Harrogate at 6.10pm. The spare engine for this duty appears to have been D20 No 1026, but on occasions two D20s were used.

After a couple of years the working was changed so that the engine on the up Pullman returned from Doncaster to Leeds (Central) on the 2.20pm slow passenger, and then ran round to Leeds City to work the 5.20pm home to Harrogate. In the reverse direction the engine off the 12.30pm Harrogate-Leeds (Central) headed the 2.2pm slow to Doncaster, returning on the 5.5pm from Doncaster (1.40pm ex Kings Cross) via Knottingley and Wetherby. The latter diagram was a reversion to earlier LNER practice, which actually went back to the days when a Great Northern engine was stationed at Starbeck.

The closure of Berwick Yard in March 1939 made a difference to the engine position on the North Main Line. Tweedmouth, which had built up an allocation of 17 K3 2-6-0s for express goods work, lost 15 of them, seven to the Scottish Area, four to Heaton, and four to York, together with two C7s to Gateshead, four B15s to Hull Dairycoates, and numerous other changes. At the same time C7 No 2194, which had been exiled at Edinburgh for about 20 years, moved to Gateshead. The four K3s transferred to York displaced four B15s to Neville Hill. The two C9 engines, by now without their boosters, were transferred from Gateshead to Tweedmouth, No 2171 on 27 May 1939 and No 727 on 19 August 1939. By all accounts Gateshead was not sorry to lose them!

Poppet valve Atlantic (ex-Uniflow) No 2212 was transferred from Gateshead to York on 29 May 1939 to join No 732, similarly rebuilt, because at this time a long drawn-out scheme was in progress to cut down the variety of engines at sheds. Where possible similar engines were gathered together at as few sheds as possible instead of being scattered indiscriminately throughout the Area.

However, transfers of Pacific engines were few and it was not until World War II had started that the largest engines began to be moved round because of the alterations in traffic flows. This commenced on 30 September 1939 when K3 No 1100, A3 Nos 2503 and 2597, and V2 No 4831 were moved from Gateshead to Heaton because of 'extra turns at Heaton and less at Gateshead due to curtailment of train services'. However, these engines still travelled on the main line and as Heaton and Gateshead often borrowed engines from one another there would be little apparent change. Six weeks later No 2503 was returned to Gateshead in exchange for A4 No 2511 as two A4s were required at Heaton: up to the outbreak of war Heaton had used their solitary A4, No 4464 *Bittern* (now preserved in running order), on the 8.15am Newcastle to Kings Cross on Mondays, Wednesdays and Fridays, returning the following days on the 10.0am from Kings Cross.

After working from Gateshead for 4½ years the high-pressure locomotive No 10000 was transferred to Neville Hill shed at Leeds on 7 January 1935. The reason for this change has not been discovered, but with the transfer of the engine to Leeds another determined attempt was made to make the engine perform satisfactorily. When the reallocation was ordered the engine was actually in Darlington Works receiving attention to the low-pressure superheater elements and it emerged on 9 January 1935, having completed some 17,000 miles since its sole General Overhaul, carried out between May 1933 and June 1934. Fifteen days later No 10000 was back in the Works again, this time to have cracks in the cylinders and steam chests welded, but at the same time the opportunity was taken to fit a double chimney and blast pipe under instructions issued by Gresley on 6 March 1935. The engine was ex-Works in its new condition on 10 May 1935 in time to take its place in an exhibition of locomotives and rolling stock held at Hunslet over the next two days, but on 22 May it was back at Darlington for minor adjustments, which took a week to carry out.

When it emerged again on 29 May it worked to Leeds hauling the dynamometer car and the counter-pressure locomotive 761, converted from a B13 4-6-0, in readiness for trials between Leeds and Hull. Test runs to Hull and back were carried out on Friday 31 May, and Tuesday, Wednesday and Thursday, 4,5 and 6 June, leaving Leeds at 10.25am and returning from Hull Dairycoates at 1.30pm. On the final day No 761 worked back to

Darlington with the dynamometer car and No 10000 remained at Leeds.

The new double-chimney arrangement caused smoke lifting problems, in spite of the sloping smokebox top and deflector wings with which the engine had been fitted when first built. Thus on 14 June No 10000 was again at Darlington, this time for 'alteration to the front end to secure smoke clearance etc', and it returned to Leeds on 10 July. During its short spell with the double chimney the engine was noted working the 9.0am Liverpool-Newcastle service between Leeds and Newcastle, returning on the 4.17pm from Newcastle: in both directions the route was via Stockton, West Hartlepool and Sunderland.

On 21 August 1935 No 10000 returned to Darlington for the last time for some light repairs to be carried out: however, before these were completed it was decided to abandon the whole project and the engine stood at North Road until 13 October 1936, when it was sent to Doncaster for rebuilding with a normal locomotive-type boiler. It was officially transferred to the Southern Area on 6 November 1937, when it was stationed at Kings Cross shed to take up its new life in its rebuilt form.

In its original form No 10000 ran approximately 90,823 miles.

In 1935-9 68 North Eastern Atlantics of the two-cylinder and three-cylinder varieties (C6 and C7) were still at work, together with the two C9 engines, although No 2171 had its booster equipment removed in December 1936 and No 727 was similarly treated in February 1937. All were painted green and Darlington Works still made an excellent job of painting them, some with Syntholux green enamel. However, after a short time in traffic they began to lose their splendour as the green paint was dulled by dirt and grime. All the Atlantics were stationed at sheds with main-line workings – York, Darlington, Gateshead, Heaton, Tweedmouth, St. Margarets (Edinburgh) and Neville Hill (Leeds), but the building of V2 engines in 1938/9 displaced some Atlantics from the main line for the first time when C6 Nos 532, 649, 698, 699, 701 and 704 were transferred to Scarborough, and Nos 700, 742, 784, 1776, 1792 and 1794 to Bridlington, in May, June and July 1939.

The withdrawal of the Raven Pacifics meant that replacement engines were required at York and Nos 2570 *Tranquil* and 2576 *The White Knight* were transferred from Gateshead in November 1936: however, it was decided that as 2576 was fitted with ACFI feed-water equipment it would be better at Gateshead, so a few weeks later it was returned to Tyneside and No 2568 *Sceptre* went to York. No 2577 *Night Hawk* followed in January 1937 and 2569 *Gladiateur* in April 1938, the latter displaced by a new A4 engine. York shed received its first A3 Pacific when No 2505 *Cameronian* was moved from Gateshead to York on 2 December 1939, but it was replaced by No 2501 *Colombo* a week later because it was considered that 2505 had too high a mileage.

Also on 2 December 1939 Leeds received three A3 Pacifics for the improved wartime passenger service which started on that day: these were Nos 2573 *Harvester* from Gateshead, and Nos 2580 *Shotover* and 2597 *Gainsborough* from Heaton. These, at long last, were the first Pacifics to be stationed at Neville Hill for the Newcastle turns – but they were only there until 28 February 1940, when they were switched to York, and once again Leeds had to use D49s on its top jobs.

For a hundred years main-line working south of York has been bedevilled by swing bridges across the River Ouse, at Naburn, four miles from York, and at Selby, where speed restrictions have always been necessary. The signalbox at Naburn was closed in 1967 and the bridge has now been fixed and can no longer be swung; but that at Selby can still be called for by vessels proceeding up or down the river. A hazard here is that passing vessels occasionally collide with the bridge or its supports, and although this has occurred on a number of occasions the bridge has not been severely damaged, unlike the bridge downstream at Goole carrying the Doncaster-Hull line, which had one span completely demolished and knocked into the river in December 1973. Another problem at Selby is expansion in the heat of the sun: if the bridge expands when open there is difficulty getting it back into place again for rail traffic and on hot days cold water has to be constantly played on to the metalwork to reduce the expansion. For many years the speed limit over the bridge was 30mph, but this has now been raised to 45mph.

Another major slack is always necessary at York, where all passenger traffic has to pass through the station, there being no avoiding lines as at Darlington. Until the extensions at York in 1938 almost all East Coast expresses were dealt with at the main up and down platforms 4 and 5, renumbered 8 and 9 respectively in 1938, both under the magnificent arched roof of the 1877 station. Newcastle-Liverpool trains were usually handled at No 14 platform, outside the wall of the original station and dating from 1900. This meant that these trains could travel on the Leeds line as far as Chaloners Whin Junction, thus avoiding any conflicting movements with Kings Cross trains. Platform 14 could be used by trains in both directions, as could 15 and 16, added in 1938.

However, the greatest change came in 1951 when the new electric signalling was brought into use: work on the resignalling had actually started prior to World War I.

The new system gave much improved facilities, and the speed with which routes could be changed was amazing: the turn of a few switches in the new box replaced numerous lever movements in the five signalboxes previously controlling the immediate station area – Locomotive Yard, Station, Leeman Road, Waterworks, and Clifton. New routes were also created and signalled, such as using No 9 platform for up expresses, facilitating cross-platform connections with trains in No 14 platform instead of forcing passengers to cross the footbridge. However, even after twenty years I still find it odd when I see an up express running into No 9 platform!

Trains not stopping at York normally passed through on the up and down main lines and, in fact, over the years a few trains not publicly booked to stop at York did halt in the middle roads to change engines or crews. The pre-1939 down 'Scarborough Flier' was one of these; the Pacific which had hauled the train from London could not be turned at Scarborough and was invariably removed from the train at York to be replaced by a 4-4-0, 4-4-2, or 4-6-0. Occasionally, when the down main was blocked, it was necessary to make other arrangements and I have seen the down 'Flying Scotsman' pass through on No 9 and No 14 platform roads; once, when both these were occupied by trains, and the down main by a light engine, I saw the down 'Scotsman' pass through on the up main, regaining the down main at the end of the platforms.

At Durham not only was the station at the end of a long, high, viaduct, but there were curves to the south (Relly Mill) and north (Newton Hall). At all three locations improvements have recently been completed to allow higher speeds.

Gateshead and Newcastle have always had restrictions because of the curve on to the King Edward Bridge at the Gateshead end (20mph), the congested area around Newcastle Central station (15mph), and the curve through Manors (25mph). The non-stop 'Flying Scotsman', and its successor 'The Elizabethan', usually ran through one of the platform roads, but the goods lines outside the station could be used if necessary. The curve at Morpeth carried a 30mph limit, and the Royal Border Bridge and through Berwick 40mph, although the restriction through Berwick station was 10mph lower in the up direction in 1925 until raised to 40mph in 1927. Over the last few years much work has been done to improve layouts and permit running at higher speeds. As limits are still being raised continually, it is probable, that some mentioned above will be out of date before this book appears in print.

Until February 1929 Pacifics were not allowed to be piloted between Berwick and Edinburgh, and even when this restriction was first lifted assistance could only be provided by 4-4-0 engines. Thus various ex-North British 4-4-0s appeared at Newcastle on such duties, together with D49s and the ex-Great Northern D1 4-4-0s stationed in Scotland. At the same time B16 4-6-0s were not allowed to be double-headed at all.

Procedure was laid down for obtaining replacement or assistant engines for East Coast expresses. In the 1930s a North Eastern Area driver gave three short whistles when passing a signalbox which was open: a driver of a Pacific in trouble and requiring assistance from Tweedmouth or Berwick gave three short and one long. Both could be cancelled by one crow (long-short-long-short-long).

New instructions issued in 1939 ordained that: 'When requiring new engine – three short. When requiring new engine but load is beyond that of one Atlantic-three short, one long. Assistant engine required-three short, one crow. Cancel-one crow'. North Eastern Area men in trouble returning from Grantham had to give the Southern Area code of three crows for a replacement engine at Doncaster.

After World War II (1955 Supplement) the standard North Eastern Region code became: one crow for assistant engine; three crows for a replacement engine; and three crows, one long to cancel. Further alterations (1960) were: assistant engine required-one crow, two longs; new engine-three crows; cancel-three short, two longs.

North of Newcastle the North British practice was continued of marshalling the assistant engine 'inside' the rostered locomotive – that is, the assistant engine was coupled to the train with the rostered engine in front. This was because the senior driver was usually to be found on the rostered engine, whereas the pilot engine might be in the charge of a 'passed fireman', ie a fireman allowed to act as driver when required. Thus as the driver of the leading engine was in charge of the train it was considered right that the senior driver should be on it. It was, however, not only the North British men who persisted in having the pilot engine next to the train, as the North Eastern men working to Edinburgh did the same. South of Newcastle this did not apply and the assistant engine was normally coupled ahead of the train engine.

The practice of frequent double-heading north of Newcastle (and particularly between Berwick and Edinburgh) led to two mishaps near Edinburgh, one in 1881 and the other in 1884, both occurring to the 8.30pm from Kings Cross. On each occasion the driver of the leading engine had no control over the continuous brake, which could only be operated by the driver of the second engine.

In August 1881, probably due to lack of co-ordination between the drivers, the rear seven vehicles broke away from the train and ran back down a 1 in 78 gradient. A fish van had been attached at Berwick, but it had been put in front of the rear brakevan, destroying the guard's control of the continuous (simple vacuum) brake; when the vehicles ran away he was unable to stop them with his handbrake in the van and they collided with a following North British train.

In August 1884 a double-headed train was slowing down for a ticket stop at Portobello when the driver of the leading engine saw an obstruction (a NB engine) on the line ahead. He could not brake his engine hard enough to stop in time, whilst the driver of the second engine, who could have stopped the train in time with the continuous brake, did not see the engine ahead of them until they hit it! Surprisingly in neither case did the Inspecting Officer condemn the practice of the leading driver not having full control of the train.

Smith's simple vacuum brake was used on East Coast Joint Stock from the 1870s, but the NER adopted the Westinghouse brake in 1878 and retained it for some 50 years. The ECJS changed over to the automatic vacuum brake. With the formation of the LNER the confusion became greater as some of the constituent companies used the Westinghouse brake and others the vacuum. It was decided to standardise the vacuum brake throughout the system (except on certain parts of the Great Eastern section) and from 1928 Westinghouse coaching stock was converted to use the vacuum brake. Westinghouse pumps were retained on many NE and NB locomotives, but they supplied air for the locomotive brakes only as the train pipes were removed.

Darlington Works ceased to fit Westinghouse pumps to new engines in 1924 and thus the K3 2-6-0s and the three North Eastern Pacifics Nos 2402-4 were turned out without Westinghouse equipment. As most freight stock was dual-braked it did not matter so much with the K3s, but the lack of Westinghouse brakes on the Pacifics proved to be inconvenient and they were fitted with Westinghouse brakes a few months after being built. Thus although the Gresley Pacifics for the GN and NB sections had only vacuum brakes the 15 engines for the North Eastern Area (Nos 2568-82) had Westinghouse equipment as built. However, this was removed in 1933-5, since the need for it disappeared as the conversion of the rolling stock was completed. Darlington Works gained from experience and in 1926-9 resumed fitting Westinghouse gear to new engines intended for use in the North Eastern Area on such classes as J39 and D49. In addition, some K3s numbered in the 13xx series and built at Darlington in 1929 were fitted.

Above right: The up 'Flying Scotsman' arriving at York with Class C6 4-4-2 No. 699 piloting Class A1 No.2571 *Sunstar.* /W. H. Whitworth

Right: Two B15 4-6-0s on a down fitted goods at Low Fell. /W. B. Greenfield

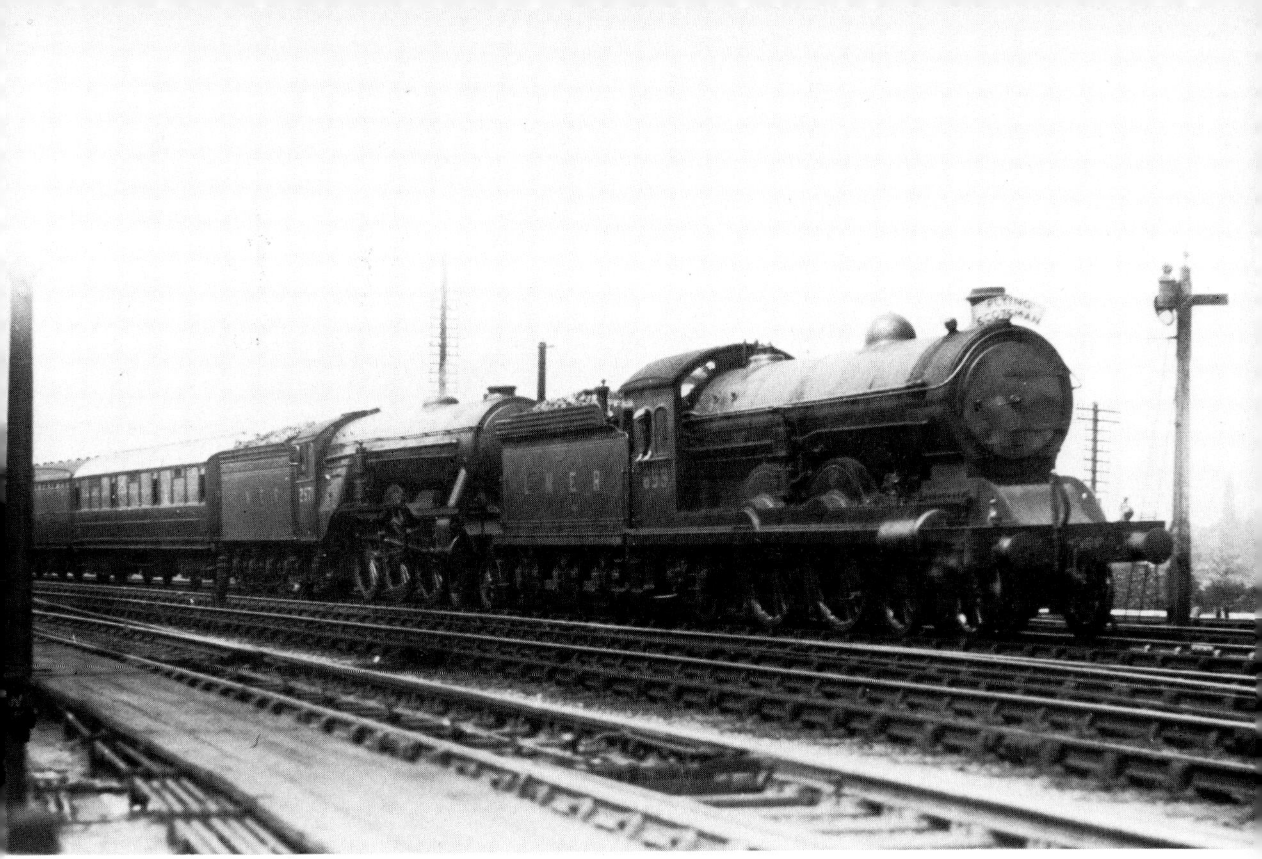
FLYING SCOTSMAN
L N E R

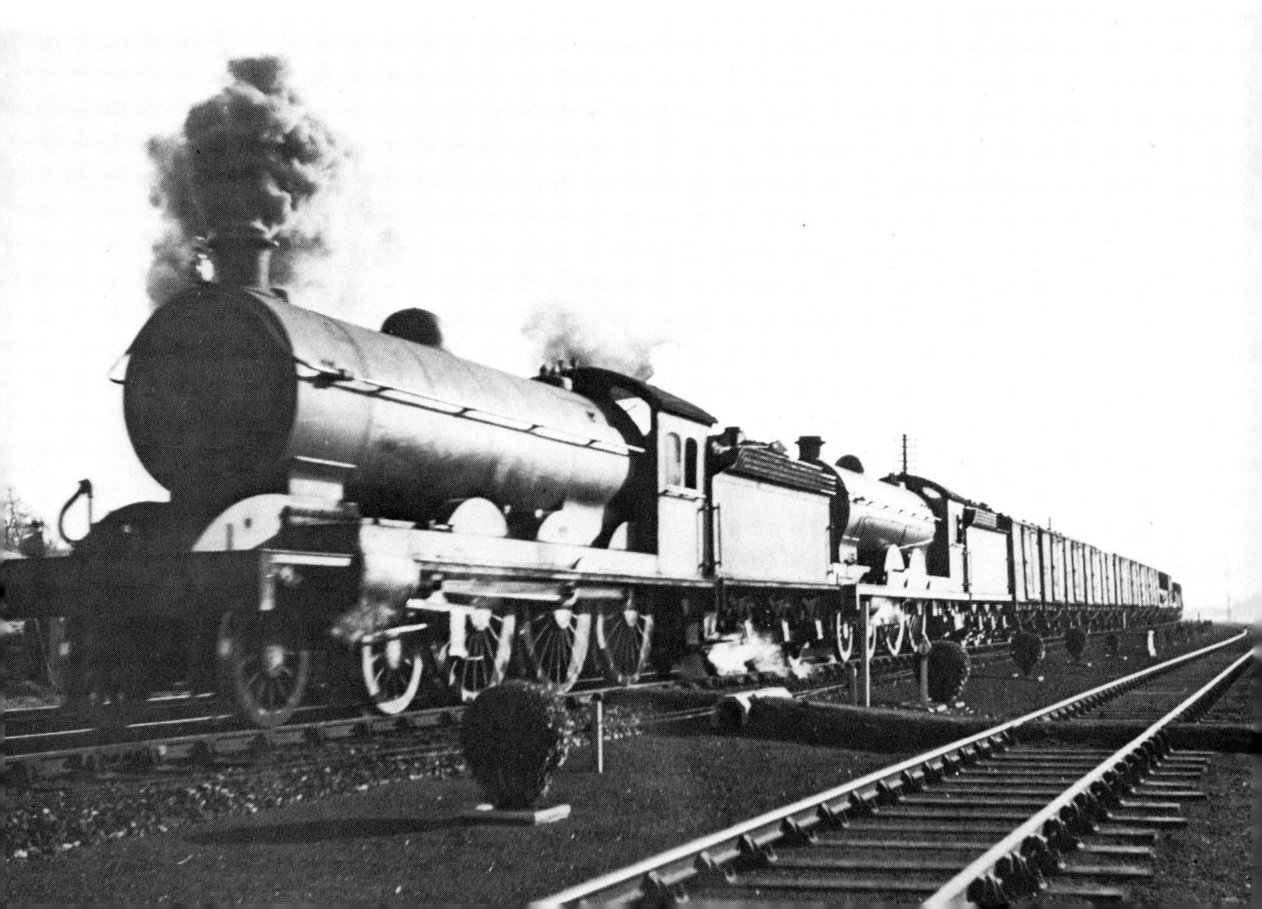

Top: Class D21 4-4-0 No. 1240 on an up express at Low Fell on 29 July 1939./*W. B. Greenfield*

Above: Class C6 4-4-2 No. 697 piloting an A1 Pacific at Low Fell./*W. B. Greenfield*

Top: Class G5 0-4-4T No. 1791 propelling an inspection saloon on the down main line at Low Fell on 26 March 1939.
/W. B. Greenfield

Above: Class C1 4-4-2 No. 4447 at Newcastle on 1 July 1943. This engine was fitted with a cut-down cab and boiler mountings for trials on the North British section. It was a York engine.
/W. B. Greenfield

49

Below: Class D2 No. 4180 and Class D3 No. 4079 – both York 4-4-0s – on a down express at Low Fell on 1 June 1936. /*W. B. Greenfield*

Bottom: Class C11 4-4-2 No. 9878 *Hazeldean* at Newcastle after arriving from Edinburgh on 8 August 1936./*W. B. Greenfield*

Right: Class B17 No. 2835 *Milton* – a Doncaster engine – at Newcastle./*W. B. Greenfield*

Below right: Armstrong-Whitworth diesel-electric locomotive on demonstration run to North Wylam on 6 July 1933./*Author's Collection*

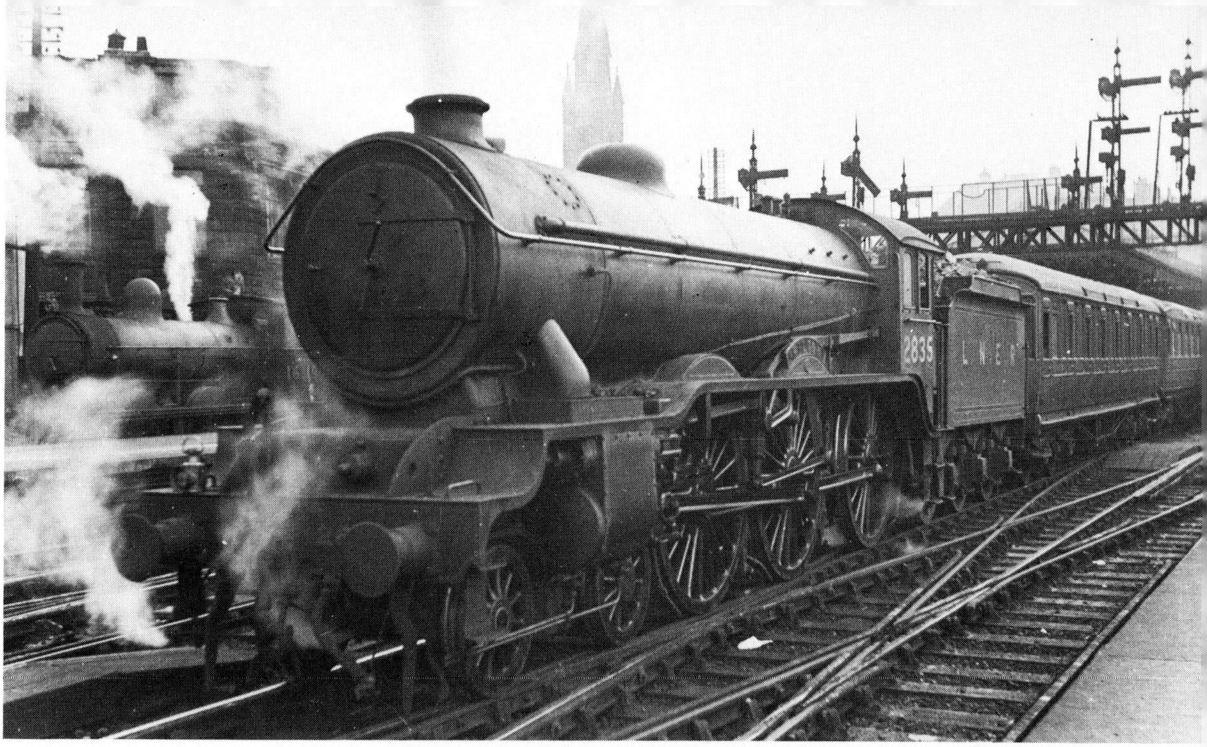
2835
L N E R

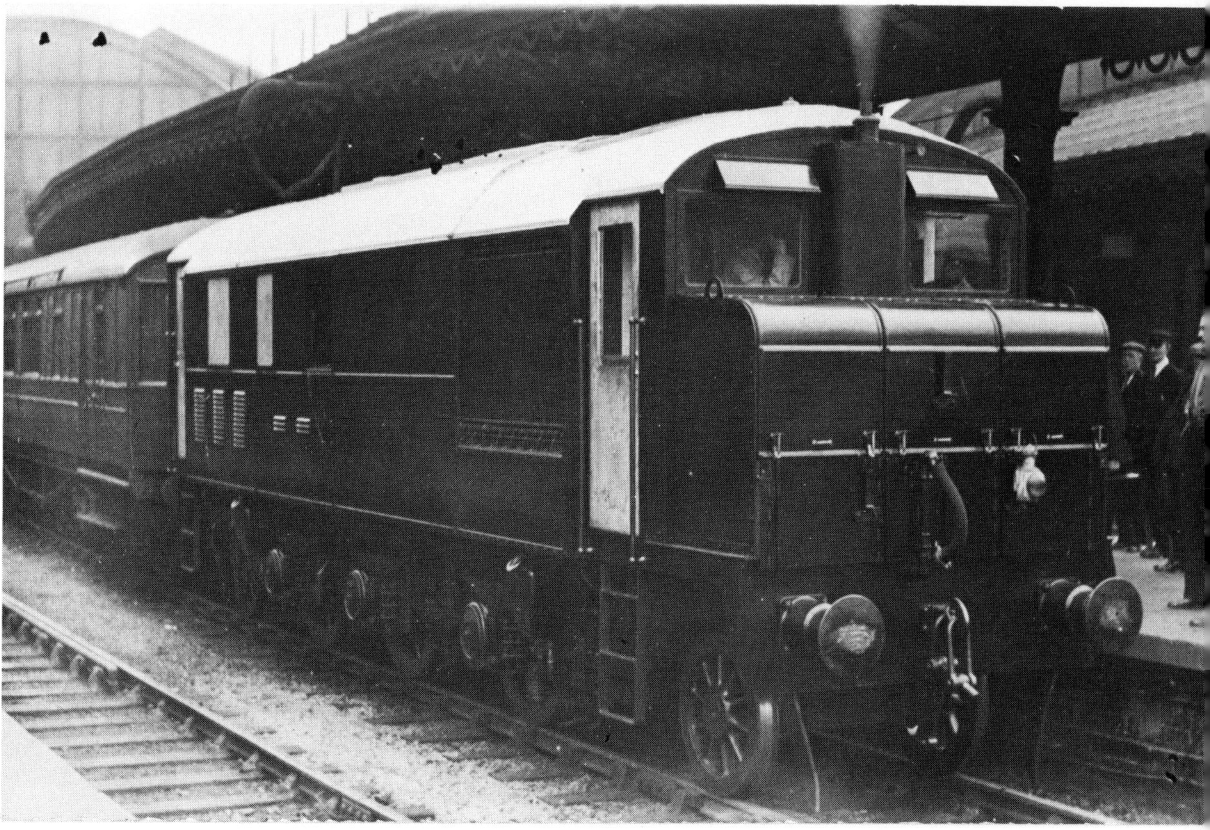

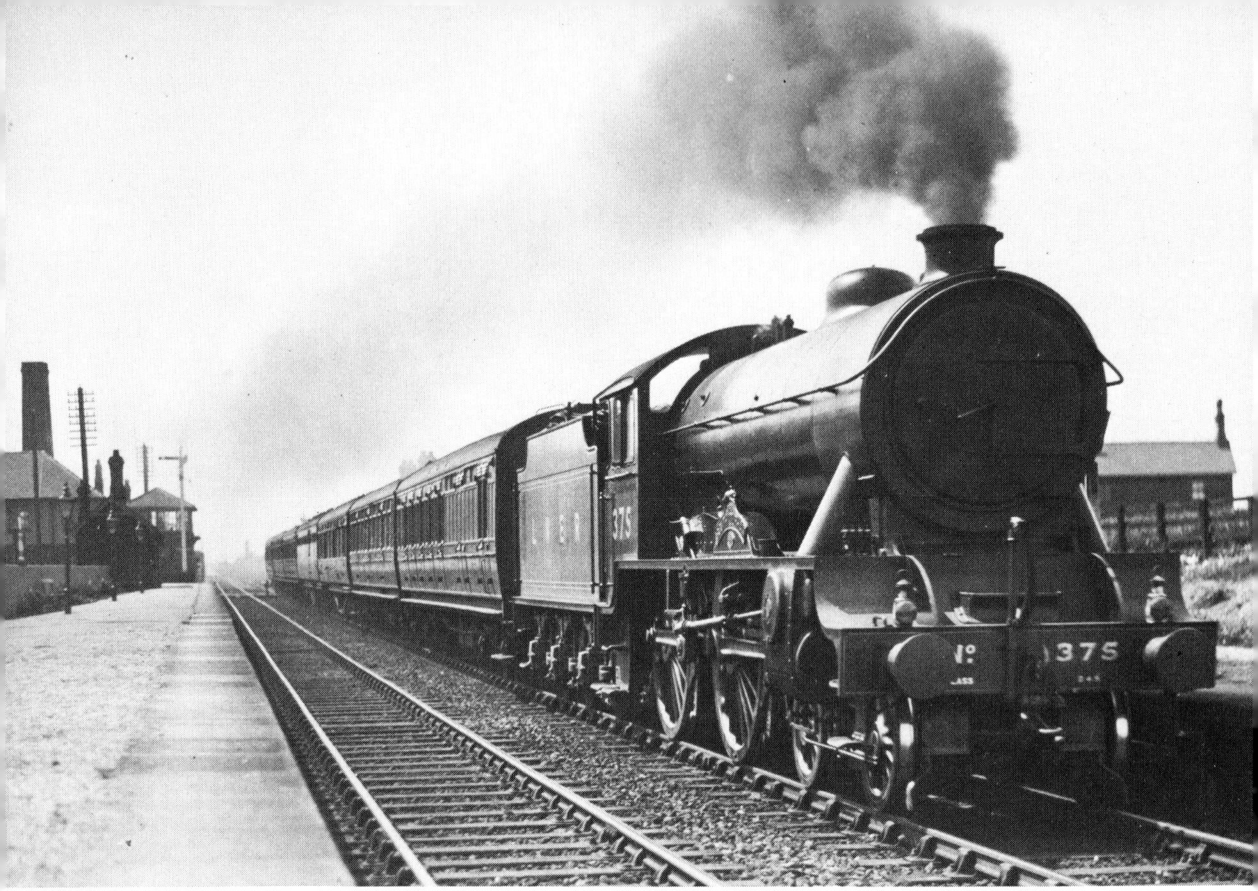
L N E R
375
No 375

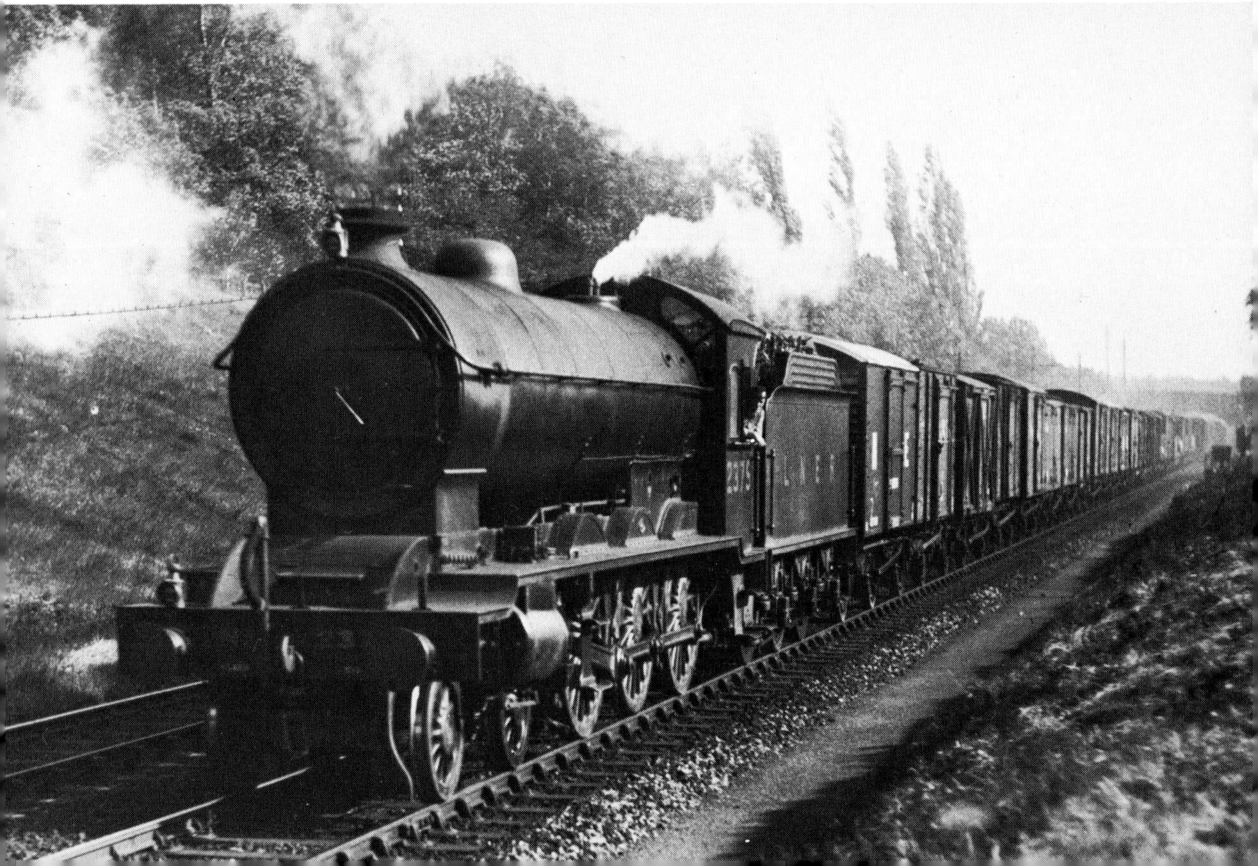
2375
L N E R

Left: Class D49/2 4-4-0 No. 375 *The South Durham* on a Liverpool-Newcastle train (LMS stock), passing Greatham. /*H. G. Tidey*

Below left: Class B16 4-6-0 No. 2375 on a down goods at Croft Spa on 8 June 1935./*W. Rogerson*

Below: Class B16 4-6-0 No. 2374 in Newcastle Central station./ *W. B. Greenfield*

Bottom: A Class Q5 0-8-0 rebuilt with Q10 boiler on an up goods at Low Fell on 3 June 1939./*W. B. Greenfield*

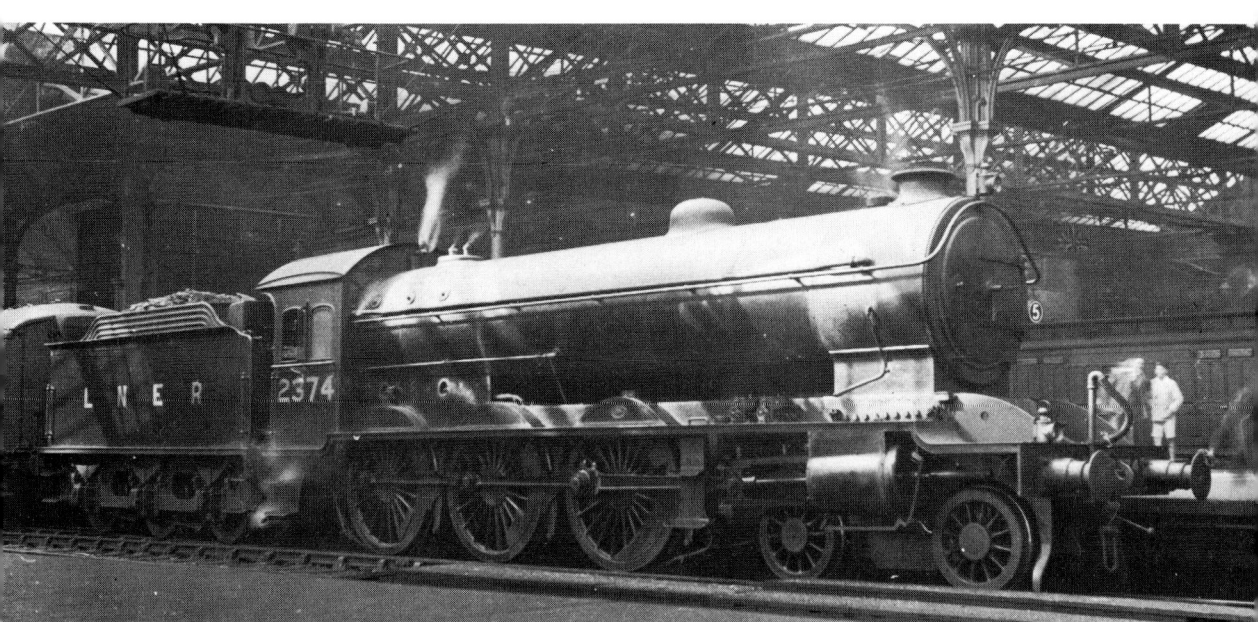

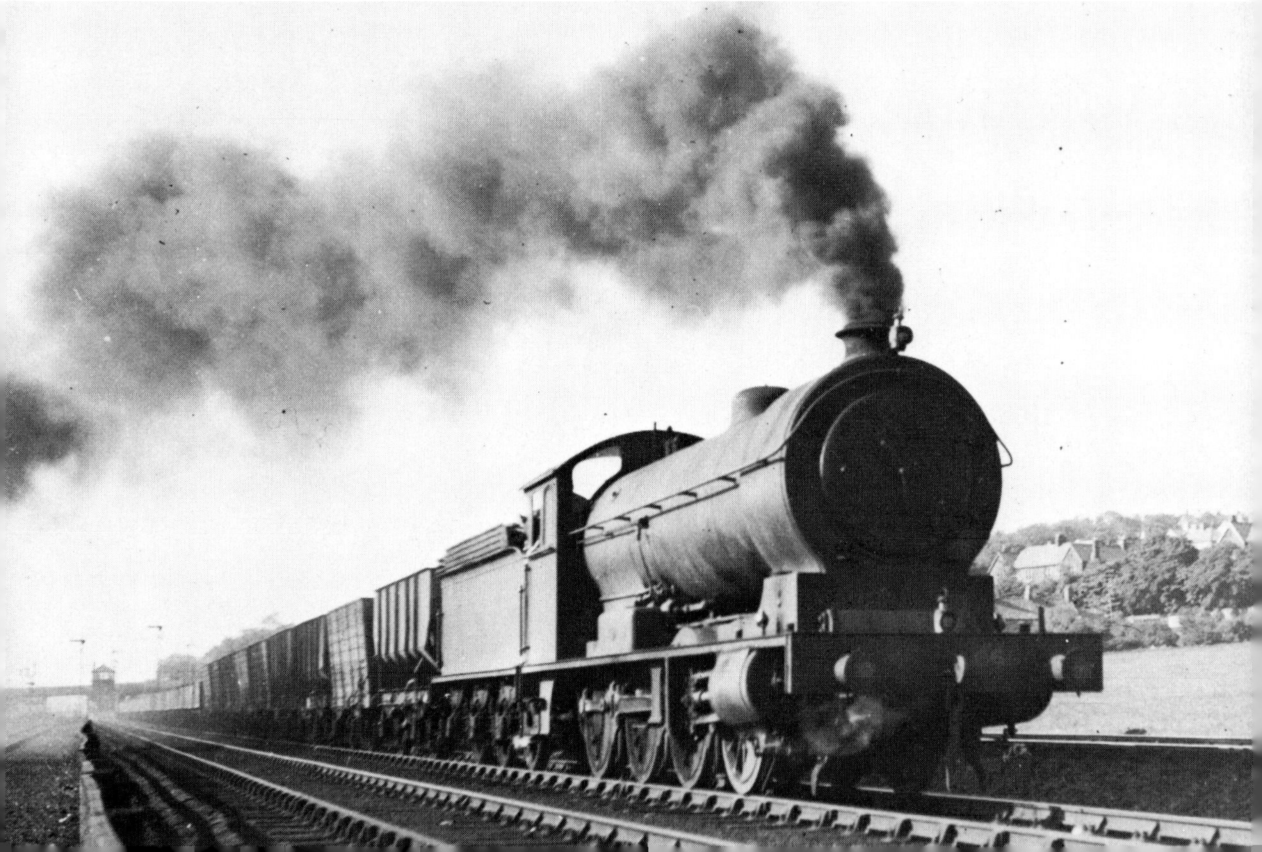

Top: Class K3 2-6-0 No. 1389 on an up goods at Northallerton.
/ *H. G. Tidey*

Above: Class A1 4-6-2 No. 2570 *Tranquil* on a 'Scouts Cruise'
train leaving York./*C. Ord*

Top: An East Coast express engine of earlier days at Newcastle – No. 1621 of Class D17/1, now preserved in York Museum. */W. B. Greenfield*

Above: Class W1 4-6-4 No. 10000 in original condition with water tube boiler, but fitted with double chimney, at Newcastle in 1935 during its last weeks of service in this condition. */W. B. Greenfield*

Above: A main-line stopping train with Class D20 No. 476 taking water at Durham on 13 May 1936./*H. C. Casserley*

Below: Class D17/2 4-4-0 No. 1923 passing Headingley on the Leeds Northern line on a down express./*Author's Collection*

Above: Class A4 4-6-2 No. 4493 *Woodcock* in green livery at York./*T. E. Rounthwaite*

Below: Class A4 No. 2509 *Silver Link* passing Croft Spa on an up express on 1 June 1936./W. Rogerson

Top: Class A4 No. 4497 *Golden Plover* at Newcastle in blue livery./*W. B. Greenfield*

Above: Class D20 4-4-0 No. 2014 on the Harrogate portion of the up 'Yorkshire Pullman' at York on 22 June 1939. /*W. B. Greenfield*

Top: Class C7 4-4-2 No. 2166 on an up fitted goods at Low Fell./ *W. B. Greenfield*

Above: Class A4 4-6-2 No. 2512 Silver Fox, in blue livery and with nameplate, entering Newcastle Central on the down 'Flying Scotsman' in 1938./*W. B. Greenfield*

Above: Class A4 4-6-2 No. 4462 *Great Snipe* on the King Edward Bridge on an up express./*British Rail*

Below: Class D49/2 4-4-0 No. 365 *The Morpeth* crossing Croxdale Viaduct on 16 February 1939./*BR*

1940-1944

World War II brought greatly increased traffic, both freight and passenger, and at times the locomotive sheds along the main line were hard pressed for locomotives, even though new engines were being built all the time (somewhat slowly because of lack of materials) and the scrapping of new engines was kept to a minimum. Thus the advent of the WD and USA 2-8-0 engines eased the position considerably and even allowed some North Eastern engines to be put into store, to be brought out again when the visitors departed for the opening of the Second Front in Europe.

Shortage of motive power led to locomotives being used more extensively, and far more former Great Northern and Great Central engines were seen north of York than ever before. This was because York, being a frontier post, received trains from the south headed by Southern Area engines due for replacement at York. If no suitable engine was available, then the engine was remanned and worked the same train forward, although what more often happened was that the engine was replaced, and if there was no suitable return working the men returned home as passengers and the engine remained at York. After fire cleaning, coaling, and watering it was then available for traffic, preferably towards its home depot, but if an engine was required urgently for a Newport or Heaton goods the non-NE engine had to go. However, LMS engines did not work north of York.

During the war great use was made of the Northallerton-Ripon-Harrogate-Leeds line, the one-time Leeds Northern, enabling freight trains between Teesside and south Yorkshire or Lancashire to reach Leeds without using the main line or York. Assistance was provided for the climb to Harrogate and a fleet of A8 4-6-2T went to Starbeck for this purpose. Troop trains also followed this route and I well remember a November night in 1943 when I was in a party of 30 which boarded such a train at New Barnet, with V2 No 4773, bound for an unknown port. The train had started further south, the accommodation which should have been reserved for us had disappeared and each compartment was occupied by two sleeping soldiers. When we asked if they were occupying our accommodation we were told in no uncertain manner where we should go! Our party

had no choice but to try and get some sleep in the leading brakevan, taking it in turns to occupy the guard's ducket seats, and when it was daylight I thought the countryside looked familiar as we plugged along behind another V2. I discovered we were somewhere between Ripon and Northallerton, apparently having travelled via Knottingley and Church Fenton. From Northallerton we continued on the main line to Newcastle, and eventually to Glasgow, where we embarked on the troopship *Highland Princess* (a prewar frozen meat carrier) – but that's another story.

Prior to this I had been working at Croft Spa, just south of Darlington, where shift duties allowed many mornings and afternoons to be spent watching main-line traffic, and from there I moved to Wrekenton, on the southern outskirts of Gateshead. From both these locations I travelled home to Scarborough every second or third weekend and was thus able to keep an eye on happenings on the main line. I well remember seeing for the first time the USA, WD, and LMS 2-8-0s, as well as the 'King Arthur' 4-6-0s from the Southern Railway.

A fireman friend of mine from my schooldays was by this time a Running Foreman at Gateshead shed and I went there regularly when he was on the evening shift and my duties permitted. At times of pressure I was enrolled to move engines in the yard – usually North Eastern Atlantics, which I preferred – but on one occasion when moving a V2 I could not find the cylinder cocks lever and some rude remarks were passed about the noise and steam filling the shed!

Extra coal trains running from the North-East to the South of England necessitated a stud of O4 2-8-0s for these duties and in 1940 Heaton collected 12 of the class and West Hartlepool got eight, from such sheds as Hull Springhead, Darlington, and Cudworth. York also acquired six of the class to work trains of Northamptonshire ironstone on to the various ironworks in the North-East. These trains were brought into York by LMS Garratts.

An involved series of transfers took place in November 1940 with the acquisition by the War Department of O4 2-8-0s from the LNER Southern Area. To help replace these the North Eastern Area supplied K3 2-6-0s from various sheds; those which went from Gateshead were replaced by three D49 4-4-0s from York, which also supplied three K3s to the Southern Area, and these were replaced at York by five D49s from Scarborough. Scarborough received two D20 4-4-0s from Leeds and three from York.

Heaton exchanged A1 No 2582 *Sir Hugo* for A4

No 4463 *Sparrow Hawk* on 26 October 1940, and on 1 August 1941 acquired A4 No 4482 *Golden Eagle* from the Scottish Area: 4462 had been renamed *William Whitelaw* at York on 24 July 1941 and as it was considered appropriate that the engine should be stationed in Scotland it was moved north in exchange for No 4482.

Tweedmouth received its first V2 in February 1944, but it was returned to Gateshead a few weeks later as it was not required for East Coast pilot work. In November of the same year Darlington shed received its first V2, when Nos 3675 and 4835 were transferred from Gateshead and York respectively for pilot duties.

April 1943 was a notable month for locomotives. The first WD 2-8-0s started arriving from the Scottish Area, where they had been run-in after delivery from the builders, the North British Locomotive Co. Ltd. The first of the 70xx series from Hyde Park Works for the North Eastern Area, Nos 7014 and 7023, went to York on 9 April 1943, followed nine days later by the first 73xx from Queen's Park Works, No 7302.

At the same time USA 2-8-0s started arriving at Darlington Works for modifications before being put into traffic. The first to emerge was No 2244, which was sent to Darlington shed for running-in on 10 May 1943, before being sent on to the LMS 14 days later. Some of the Darlington-modified engines were handed to the North Eastern Area, the final allocation being 25 engines at both Heaton and Neville Hill. Henceforward the WD and USA types became common on the main line until the latter were recalled for use in Europe in September 1944.

Another class of 2-8-0 new to the northern part of the Area (they had been working to York off the LMS for some time) were the Stanier 2-8-0s, of which No 8510 (built at Doncaster) went to Heaton on 8 February 1944, to be joined 11 days later by No 8500 (built at Darlington).

Also to be seen on the main line were two B4 4-4-0s from the Southern Railway, Nos 2051 and 2068, which arrived at Leeds on 14 November 1941. After some months working between Leeds, York, Thirsk, and Northallerton, they were transferred to York on 11 July 1942. A regular job for one of them was on the 10.5am York-Newcastle, on which they were used as pilot to a North Eastern or Great Northern Atlantic: the engines returned together on a Newcastle-York parcels train. They were returned to the Southern on 1 December 1944 as 'not required'.

The next batch of strangers comprised ten 'King Arthur' 4-6-0s, also from the Southern Railway (Nos 739/40/2/4/7-51/4), which arrived at Heaton in

November 1942. They were used mainly on the North main line to Tweedmouth and Edinburgh, but they also worked to York, Leeds, and Hull, usually on freight trains. Eight of the class were returned to the Southern in the first fortnight of July 1943, consequent upon the allocation of USA 2-8-0s to Heaton, and the remaining two (Nos 742 and 750) followed on the last day of July.

Also new on the North Eastern scene were the B1 4-6-0s, of which the first, No 8301 *Springbok*, commenced working between Darlington and Leeds in December 1942, followed by Nos 8302-10 over the next eighteen months. These engines were run-in at Darlington and then despatched to other sheds, mostly outside the North Eastern Area.

New V2s were appearing frequently from Darlington and Doncaster and after No 4899 was completed in January 1942 a new series commenced at 3641 and ran to 3695, eventually totalling 184 engines. There is no need for me to stress the fine work these engines performed in World War II, not only on heavy freight trains, but also on expresses of unprecedented size of 20 or more coaches.

Sir Nigel Gresley had died in 1941 and was succeeded by Edward Thompson, who soon put his own ideas into practice. The B1 4-6-0s have already been mentioned and next his attention turned towards improving the Gresley V2 by turning out the final four of the order as 4-6-2 engines. The first of this ugly quartet was No 3696, outshopped from Darlington in May 1944 and sent to Bank Top shed for running-in. On 8 June it moved to Heaton for testing on the 9.20am Newcastle-Leeds-York-Newcastle diagram, leaving the North Eastern Area for Kings Cross on 10 November. The second engine, No 3697, went new to Darlington shed on 30 June for running-in, but spent five months under the eye of North Road Works before going to Kings Cross on 25 November. The third engine, No 3698, spent almost four months working from Darlington before being sent to the Scottish Area on 14 March 1945, followed a couple of weeks later by No 3699, which spent only six weeks at Bank Top. One of Thompson's rebuilds, No 2003 *Lord President*, was stationed at Gateshead shed for trials in February and March 1945. Other Thompson rebuilds which could be seen on the main line, usually on freight workings, were the rebuilt B16s, commencing with No 922 in May 1944, and the sole two-cylinder D49, No 365 *The Morpeth*.

On 28 March 1943 a massive redistribution of engines took place in the North Eastern Area as a result of the changed position brought about by the war. Many of the transfers involved the smaller goods engines, both tender and tank, but a number of main line engines were affected, of which the most notable were:

11 A3 to Heaton (6 from Gateshead and five from York)
31 V2 to Gateshead (23 from Heaton and 8 from York)
44 J39 to Darlington
A11 69 B16 to be stationed at York.

The most drastic move was the reduction in status of the North Eastern Atlantics. Hull Dairycoates received two C6 and 22 C7 for goods workings on the former North Eastern lines radiating from Hull, whilst Hull Springhead received ten C6, and Cudworth two C6, for mineral workings over former Hull & Barnsley lines.

Interior of York station after the bombing in April 1942. Note the underframes of the sleeping car train destroyed by fire in platform 9./*BR*

Top: Class C7 4-4-2 No. 2204 leaving Low Fell Yard with an up goods banked in the rear, on 27 May 1940./*W. B. Greenfield*

Above: Class Q5 0-8-0 No. 1717 leaving Low Fell Yard on 27 January 1940, in the first winter of World War II./*W. B. Greenfield*

64

Top: A Class C7 Atlantic and a Class A1 Pacific on an up express at Low Fell in February 1941./*W. B. Greefield*

Above: Class K3 2-6-0 No. 1307 on a down ambulance train passing Low Fell on 27 May 1940./*W. B. Greenfield*

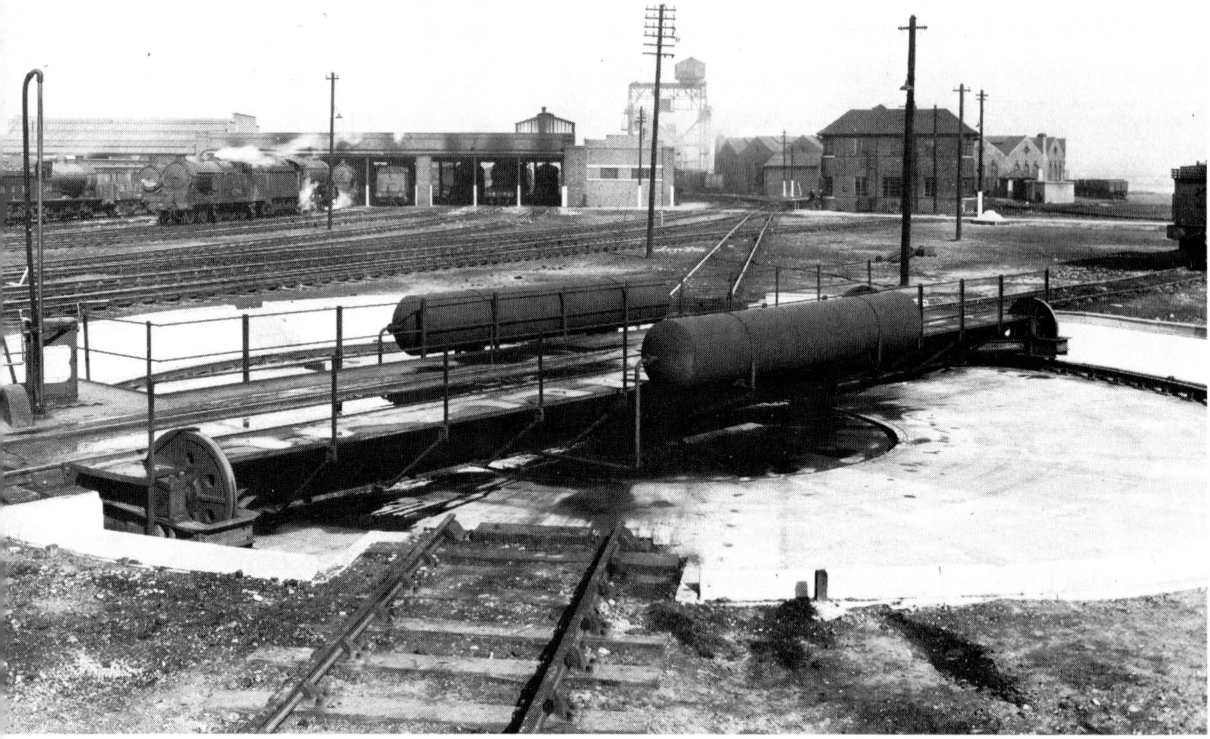

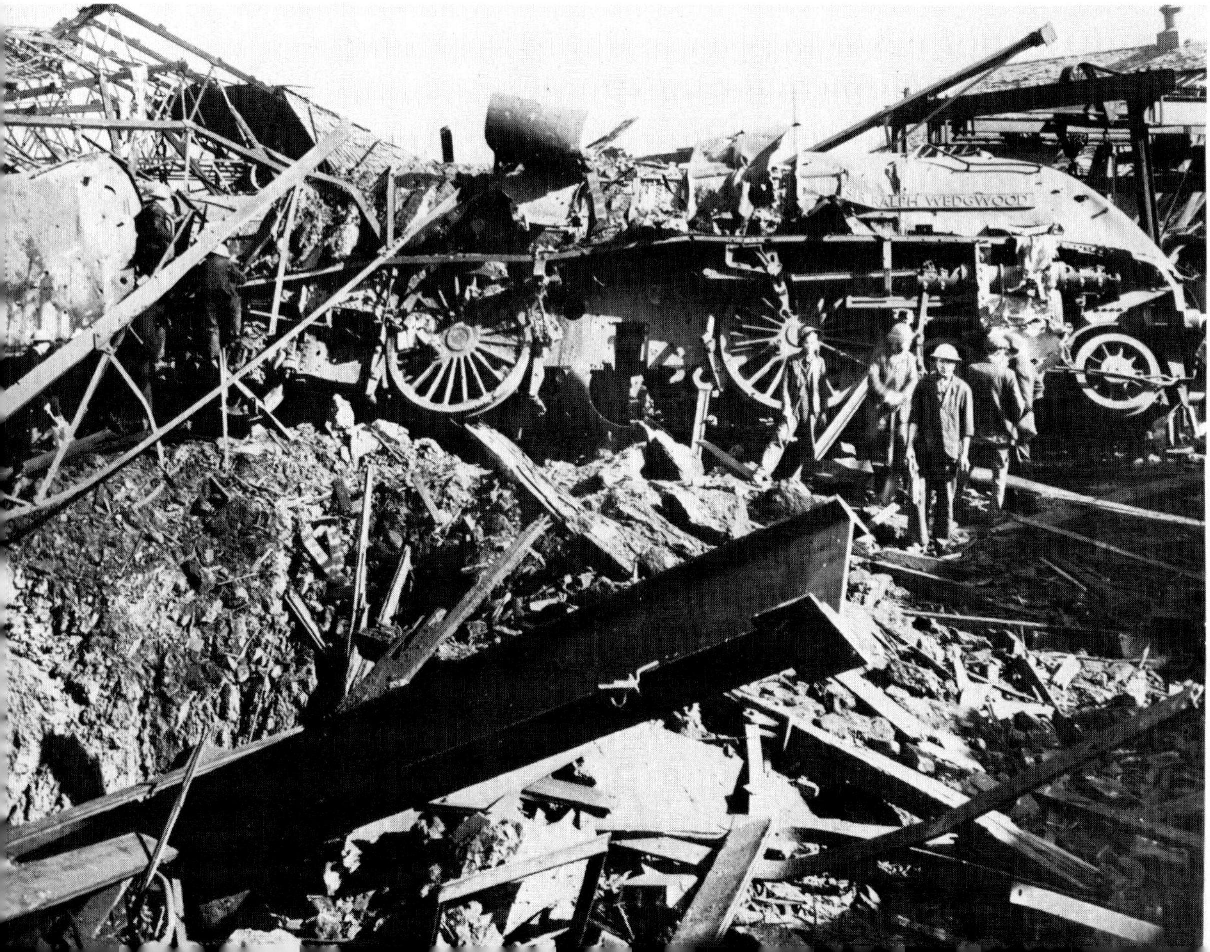
SIR RALPH WEDGWOOD

Left: The south end of Darlington shed on 2 October 1940. Note the vacuum turntable in the foreground. The rebuilding of Darlington shed was completed just prior to the outbreak of World War II./*BR*

Below left: Interior of York shed after the bombing with damaged A4 No. 4469 *Sir Ralph Wedgwood./BR*

Below: WD 2-8-0 No. 77145 at Darlington after war service./*BR*

Centre: Class 8F 2-8-0 No. 8500 built at Darlington in 1944 and allocated to Heaton./*BR*

Bottom: USA 2-8-0 No. 2032 as modified at Darlington for service in Great Britain./*BR*

1945-1949

The end of the war found the railways struggling along after their magnificent work in keeping running the country's transport system. I was in Italy at the time and on 8 May, the official end of hostilities, I was in charge of a small Signals detachment under canvas some 20 miles north of Rome and we spent the day glued to our radio sets. At night we fired nearly all our ammunition into the air in celebration! Leave came later in the year, involving a 42hour journey in a Hungarian coach through Austria, Germany, and France on the first leave train to run from Villach to Calais.

Between 1946 and 1949 I travelled from Kings Cross to York and back every alternate week-end – down on the 5.30pm ex-Kings Cross on Fridays and back on the 9.30am from York on Mondays, and thus had my fill of runs behind numerous Pacifics, V2s, and No 10000. A few – very few, in fact – arrivals were two or three minutes before time but most trips, especially in the up direction, were 20-40 minutes late into Kings Cross. Unfortunately at this time I travelled very little north of York, although I did see what was working into York from Newcastle. The 5.30pm from Kings Cross was worked from Grantham by a Heaton engine and I still remember the unexpected sight of No 2582 *Sir Hugo*, resplendent once again in spotless LNER green, standing in the engine bay waiting to take over from V2 No 4823.

At this period engines were appearing with strange numbers, with the LNER renumbering scheme in full swing throughout 1946. You could see an engine on Saturday with its familiar number in correct-size shaded transfer numerals, but on Monday the same engine could be noted with a rectangular black panel where the old number had been obliterated; in its place was its new number in a style which bore no resemblance to any standard other than the painter's! Private decorators were called in to renumber some of the engines and it was easy to tell by the standard of the workmanship if they were experienced signwriters or apprentices!

In April 1946 hordes of new B1 4-6-0 engines commenced to appear from the North British Locomotive Company, commencing with No 1040 *Roedeer*. The first 20 went to the Great Eastern section, but Neville Hill got Nos 1060, 1065, 1068 and 1069, and for the first time for many years 4-6-0s could be seen on Leeds-Newcastle trains.

Those delivered up to November 1946 were turned out black, but a change to green livery was made with No 1094, and a few of the earlier engines were repainted in green before lined black became the standard BR livery for mixed traffic 4-6-0s.

Most of the early engines were stationed off the North Eastern Area, although Nos 1072, 1076 and 1081 were at Haymarket shed. At the same time Darlington Works commenced to build B1 engines and turned out No 1010 *Wildebeeste* in November 1946. Although this B1 went to Botanic Gardens shed at Hull most of the succeeding engines were allocated to main line sheds: Gateshead had Nos 1011-14; Heaton Nos 1019-23; York Nos 1015-8/34/5; Tweedmouth Nos 1024/5; and Darlington Nos 1037-9. With Gill Sans letters and figures these engines looked very smart. Although they were not intended to be top-link main-line engines they were so used for a time because of their new condition. Many York drivers preferred a new B1 to a run-down V2 for a trip to Newcastle and back if the load was not too heavy. However, their main use was on the more important branches – Leeds-York-Scarborough; Leeds-Selby-Hull; Newcastle-Carlisle, etc.

Also in 1946 the first new Thompson Pacifics appeared. The earlier rebuilding of the P2 2-8-2 Nos 2001-6 in 1943/4, and of No 4470 *Great Northern* in 1945, had warned us what might be expected. The North Eastern Area's original allocation of Thompson Pacifics was Gateshead: Nos 500/11/2/8/21/2 (but No 500 soon moved to Kings Cross, Nos 511/2 to Heaton, and No 522 to York); Heaton Nos 515/6/7 (later supplemented by Nos 511/2 from Gateshead); York No 524 (plus No 522 from Gateshead); whilst Haymarket received No 519. Delivery of these A2/3 engines was completed in September 1947 and in December they were followed by the Peppercorn version (A2) Nos 525-60539 (during the building of these engines the BR numbering scheme was introduced by which all LNER engines had 60,000 added to their numbers). York received Nos 526, 60532/4/5; Gateshead Nos 527/8/31 and No 60538; Heaton No 60539; and Haymarket No 529. The last engine, No 60539 *Bronzino*, was turned out in August 1948 with a double blastpipe and chimney, and Nos 60526/9/32/3/8 were subsequently rebuilt with double chimneys and multiple-valve regulators.

Also in August 1948 the first A1 Pacific appeared and of these 22 were allocated to the North Eastern Region and five to the Scottish Region. The individual allocations were:

York Nos 60121/9/38/40/1/53
Gateshead Nos 60115/24/32/5/7/42/3/5/7/51/4/5
Heaton Nos 60116/26/7/50
Haymarket Nos 60152/9/60/1/2.

Darlington built Nos 60130-52, and Nos 60114-29 and 60153-62 were constructed at Doncaster. The engines not listed above were stationed at Eastern Region sheds, but many of them worked into the North Eastern Region.

After the rebuilding of the Gresley P2 2-8-2 engines into Pacifics (A2/2) by Thompson in 1943/4 the six engines were returned to Scotland, but at the end of 1949 it was decided to transfer them to England; Nos 60501/2/3 moved to York and Nos 60504/5/6 to Peterborough (New England). In exchange Peterborough sent to Scotland A2 Nos 60530/6 and A2/1 No 60507, and York A2 Nos 60532/4/5. Neither York nor New England were top-flight main-line sheds with much long-distance express passenger work and so the displaced engines settled down to a subordinate main-line existence, not normally getting on to the top jobs and confined to workings which could just as well be handled by a V2. It was on such duties that they continued to work until they were withdrawn between November 1959 and April 1961.

After the war many of the WD 2-8-0s which had seen service overseas were returned to this country and used by the main-line companies. The LNER purchased 200 and renumbered them 3000-3199. After an overhaul and a repaint they looked positively glamorous compared with some of those still bearing wartime markings and running with their WD numbers. Eventually, of course, BR took over many more and these, together with the LNER engines, were renumbered 90000-90732.

By 1945 the North Eastern Atlantics were beginning to show their age. With the building of numerous V2 2-6-2 engines the Atlantics were to be seen less and less on the main line, confining their duties to branch lines. One such service was that between Scarborough, York and Leeds in the period 1945 to 1948. In March 1945 Scarborough's miscellaneous collection of A6, D20, D49 and J21 engines was moved away and in place C7 Nos 706, 720, 728, 729, 732, 737 arrived from York, and Nos 2207 and 2211 from Dairycoates. The Atlantics were allocated to regular crews. Before long they had been pulled round mechanically, and with well merited attention from the Scarborough cleaners, they began to uphold the North Eastern flag once again as they passed through York. Their cleanliness was a notable feature and inevitably compared very favourably with the filthy state of the main-line engines. Altogether 15 C7 Atlantics

passed through the hands of the Scarborough crews; as one engine was withdrawn another took its place until the last one departed for scrapping in November 1948. This was No 2992, old No 2207, a Leeds favourite prior to the introduction of the D49s, and the engine which represented the class in the 1925 Railway Centenary Procession. It was survived by one other member of the class – No 2970, old No 2164, which was withdrawn from Dairycoates on 27 December 1948. This was the engine involved in the disastrous head-on collision at Darlington in 1928.

In 1945 it became apparent that the war really had ended. No 1 braked freight trains were reinstated and with the winter timetable from 1 October the down 'Flying Scotsman' was accelerated by 50 minutes, arriving at Edinburgh at 6.5pm: the 5.30pm Kings Cross to Newcastle arrived 84 minutes earlier, and the 8.20pm to Edinburgh 101 minutes earlier. The restaurant cars on the 'Scotsman' (and many other trains) were restored at the same time after having been withdrawn since 9 December 1941, and the LNER even announced that it hoped to reintroduce the 'Silver Jubilee' train, but that hope did not materialise.

A few locomotives lost their wartime black livery, commencing with two Southern Area engines – the Thompson rebuild of No 4470 *Great Northern*, which became royal blue, and No 4496 *Dwight D. Eisenhower*, which was restored to garter blue. The full lettering LNER was resumed in place of the wartime NE, and the LNER announced that *all* locomotives would be painted green. In August 1946 a start was made with A3 No 2582 *Sir Hugo*, and as a token for the other classes some North Eastern Area engines were repainted green at Doncaster Works – K3 No 1935, V2 No 4854, and V3 No 7684. Unfortunately the scheme was not implemented for the older and smaller engines, although in Scotland Cowlairs and Inverurie Works managed to turn out a number of repainted green engines. The A4 Pacifics were turned out in garter blue and new Pacifics in green. Two ex-North Eastern tank engines were specially painted green in 1947 for shunting at York and Newcastle stations: J71 No 8286 for York and J72 No 8680 for Newcastle Central.

In 1946 Edward Thompson retired and was succeeded by A. H. Peppercorn.

In addition to the general acceleration of train services certain prestige trains were reintroduced, commencing with the 'Yorkshire Pullman' on 4 November 1946, but this created some ill-feeling and it was considered by some to be a wasteful luxury. Due to the bad weather and the severe restrictions on fuel the train was cancelled from 14 February 1947, but reinstated on 6 October 1947. As the patrons returned to the 'Yorkshire Pullman' it was increased to seven cars from Harrogate to Leeds Central – the pre-1939 route via York was not reintroduced – and by 1949 it was rostered to be worked by two Starbeck 4-4-0 engines, a D49 and a D20. The same two engines then worked the 1.44pm from Leeds City to Northallerton, but the D20 came off at Harrogate and after locomotive duties at Starbeck, and a change of crew, headed the 4.40pm to Leeds and returned assisting another D49 on the 'Yorkshire Pullman' at 9.26pm from Leeds Central.

The non-stop 'Flying Scotsman' was restored on 31 May 1948, with a timing of 7 hours 50 minutes in both directions. The engines used were A4 Pacifics and No 60034 *Lord Faringdon* hauled the first down train and No 60009 *Union of South Africa* the up. The working was shared between Kings Cross and Haymarket crews and North Eastern Area men were not involved. The return of the 'Scotsman' restored the long-distance locomotive workings which had been eroded by the war: in 1945/6 the longest regular diagrams had been London-York (188 miles) and Grantham-Newcastle (163 miles) as lodging turns had been abolished during the war so that crews could spend each night at home. However, as lodging turns were again introduced there was some opposition from the footplate staff, leading to the strike in the Newcastle area on 15 May 1949 and subsequent Sundays.

On 5 July 1948 the 'Queen of Scots' Pullman was restored, leaving Kings Cross at 11.30am and arriving Glasgow at 9.22pm. The train used the pre-war route via Leeds (Central), where it reversed, Harrogate, Darlington and Newcastle, and in the North Eastern Region the first down train from Leeds was worked by No 60512 *Steady Aim* of Heaton, with V2 60815 borrowed by Neville Hill for the up working. At that time the Leeds engine travelled down on the 5.18am slow from Leeds City, via Harrogate and Northallerton, and the Heaton engine and crew worked the 10.10am Newcastle-Liverpool as far as Leeds. However, after Neville Hill received Pacifics again in February 1949 (Nos 60036/74/81/6) the diagram was changed and the outward Leeds working was on the 8.48am to Newcastle via York, the train which was named the 'North Briton' later the same year. After working back to Leeds on the up Pullman the engine ran to Neville Hill shed in readiness for working the 8.35pm No 1 Braked Goods from Wellington Street to Stockton and the 12.30am return, due at Neville Hill at 3.5am. Until the arrival of the Pacifics Neville Hill normally used B1 4-6-0s on the Pullman working.

For the winter 1949 timetable the Heaton men off the Newcastle-Liverpool train still worked the down 'Queen of Scots', but with a Neville Hill A3, and the Leeds crew for the up 'North Briton' (8.21pm from Newcastle) manned the Heaton engine on the 4.40pm ex Leeds, a Liverpool-Newcastle train, regaining the Leeds engine at Newcastle. This allowed more time for the Heaton engine to be prepared at Leeds for its return working, and similarly for the Leeds engine at Newcastle. The Leeds engine on the down 'Queen of Scots' had previously worked the 5.40am to Darlington (via Harrogate) light engine to Northallerton, and the 10.5am Northallerton-Leeds. The third Leeds Pacific in daily use hauled the 11.29am Leeds-Newcastle (ex Liverpool), assisted by a Starbeck engine as far as Harrogate, and the 4.15 Newcastle-Liverpool, assisted by a Starbeck engine from Ripon to Leeds, The Starbeck engines were usually D20 or D49 4-4-0s, or J39 0-6-0s. The long-established routing via Wetherby of the 4.15pm Newcastle-Liverpool was abolished in 1948 and the train took the Arthington route henceforward.

In the summer of 1948 the first of the new Peppercorn A1 Pacifics was put into traffic, commencing at No 60114, and the second and third were allocated to the North Eastern Region – No 60115 to Gateshead and No 60116 to Heaton. The 'Tees-Tyne Pullman' started running on 27 September 1948, taking the place of the pre-war 'Silver Jubilee', leaving Newcastle at 9.0am (one hour earlier than the 'Jubilee') and arriving at Kings Cross at 2.16pm (16 minutes later): the two-minute stop at Darlington remained the same! Heaton worked the train in both directions and at first borrowed No 60115 from Gateshead as No 60116 had not arrived. However, in 1949 the working was altered so that Kings Cross men, with an A1 or A4 Pacific covered the down train and lodged overnight at Newcastle, returning to London the next morning on the up train – an arrangement which persisted for many years.

An unusual coach used in the 'Flying Scotsman' train in 1948 was the 'Silver Princess', built in America and sponsored by the Pressed Steel Co. Ltd. as a commercial venture. The sides of the coach were constructed of stainless steel sheets, hence the name, and the accommodation comprised 18 seats in three first-class compartments, and 48 seats in an open third-class saloon. General lighting was by fluorescent tubes, double glazing was fitted to the windows, and the body was sound-proofed.

The 'Flying Scotsman' ran non-stop for only one summer after the war, for on 23 May 1949 a new train was introduced, leaving Kings Cross at 9.30am and Edinburgh Waverley at 9.45am, running non-stop in eight hours in each direction, and carrying the name 'The Capitals Limited'. The method of working was exactly the same as on the non-stop 'Flying Scotsman' and, in fact, the same coaches were used. The engines in charge on the first day were the reliable A4s – No 60010 *Dominion of Canada* on the down train and No 60027 *Merlin* on the up. The 'Flying Scotsman', which during the previous winter (1948/9) had stopped only at Grantham and Newcastle, now stopped at York also and was allowed 8 hours 28 minutes for the London-Edinburgh journey; it still started at 10.0am from both capitals.

In the post-war period there were some unfortunate derailments and collisions on the East Coast main line, involving seven V2s and two Pacifics. Four of these accidents occurred within 20 miles of Kings Cross, namely the derailments involving V2 No 3645 at Hatfield and V2 No 905 at Marshmoor in 1946, and A2/1 No 60508 at New Southgate in 1948, and the collision at Potters Bar in 1946 in which V2s Nos 4833 and 4876 were involved; V2 No 4876 in the Potters Bar collision in February 1946 was the same engine as No 905 in the Marshmoor derailment in the following November! There was also a disastrous rear-end collision at Doncaster in July 1948 in which V2 936 was involved.

In the North Eastern Area V2 No 4895 was at the head of the 11.15pm from Kings Cross when at 5.40am on 5 January 1946 it ran into the wreckage of an up freight train at Browney signalbox, south of Durham. The freight train had become divided due to a broken coupling and the signalman stopped the engine (B16 4-6-0 No 842) and the front portion of the train to inform the driver what had happened. What the signalman did not realise was that at his box the main line was on a falling gradient for southbound trains, and while the front portion was stationary the rear portion of the train ran into it, derailing several wagons and fouling the down line. The down express was approaching under clear signals, and although attempts were made to stop it they were unsuccessful because some of the derailed wagons were resting on the signal wires and holding at clear the down home and distant signals.

The V2 and the leading coaches were derailed and the coaches ploughed into a field on the west side of the line. The second, third and fourth were piled in a heap and wrecked, the bodies being destroyed and the underframes seriously distorted,

with the fifth coach, considerably damaged, on top of them. Ten passengers were killed, and one soldier who had been helping in the rescue operations died from alcoholic poisoning after drinking spirits that were being carried in some of the wagons of the goods train.

Another V2 involved in a derailment was No 4878 on Sunday 24 February 1946. The engine and 10 coaches of the 6.50pm Newcastle-Bristol mail came to grief near Thirsk as the train was running slowly over track which had been relaid earlier in the day. There were no casualties.

The next accident also took place on a Sunday, 26 October 1947, the train being the 11.15am from Edinburgh to London hauled by the unlucky Pacific *Merry Hampton*, which had been involved in the deliberate derailment at Cramlington in 1926. The site was Goswick, where NER Class S No 2005 came to grief in the same way in 1907.

On this fateful day in 1947 engineering work was being carried out on the main line south of Goswick and all up traffic was being worked on the independent line, reached via a turnout at the south end of Goswick station; north of the station there were only two tracks. As the driver approached Goswick he missed seeing the distant signal at caution, and although at first the signalman kept his home signal at danger he cleared it when he thought that the driver had the train under control and was slowing for the diversion off the main line. As it happened the driver did not know that he was to be turned from up main to up independent at Goswick. When he saw the home signal at clear he mistakenly thought that he had a clear road. By the time he saw the splitting starting signals indicating that he was going on to the slow road it was too late to do anything and the engine was derailed at speed into the field on the up side of the line, in exactly the same place as No 2005 40 years earlier! A number of coaches piled up in the field behind the engine, but one (actually the first-class portion of a triplet restaurant car) continued forward on its own and came to rest on its side 54yds ahead of the engine. The coaches were carrying 'Flying Scotsman' boards as the set was the previous day's 10.0am from Kings Cross, due to return from London as Monday's 'Flying Scotsman.'

An odd feature of the accident was that there was an unauthorised passenger on the footplate – a naval stoker, clad in overalls, who had persuaded the driver to give him a ride to Newcastle and back. The Inspecting Officer suggested that the reason why the driver missed seeing the late notice about the engineering works was because he was preoccupied in getting his stoker friend into

Haymarket shed and on to the engine without being seen. One train attendant and 27 passengers were killed.

On 10 February 1949 another collision occurred on the crossing at the north end of York station, when 5MT No 4781 off the 10.8am from Manchester Victoria collided with J25 No 5656 on a Foss Islands goods.

As the 7.30pm Edinburgh-Kings Cross train was approaching the 266yds-long Penmanshiel Tunnel (between Cockburnspath and Grantshouse, north of Berwick) on 23 June 1949, a fine and warm summer evening, a fierce fire developed in the tenth coach – a fairly new corridor brake composite. The fire was at first thought to have been due to slipshod electric wiring installed by the contractors who built the vehicle, but two months after the fire it was discovered that a Doncaster driver travelling as a passenger and returning from his holidays had actually seen the fire start where there was no wiring. His evidence pointed to the surface of the corridor panelling and it transpired that the interior of the coach had been sprayed with three coats of highly inflammable clear cellulose lacquer!

Once ignited by a match or a scrap of burning paper the flames spread with amazing rapidity, and one passenger said that the flames chased him up the corridor as he retreated. Dense choking fumes were also given off. A party of three Americans was unable to escape from their compartment via the door; they broke the window on the opposite side and jumped out on to the track whilst the train was still in motion.

Fortunately, as it was a brake composite the vacuum brake valve was easily accessible and the Doncaster driver rushed into the van and destroyed the vacuum with A3 No 60035 and the leading eight coaches inside Penmanshiel Tunnel. The burning coach, and the one ahead which also caught fire, were outside the tunnel. In spite of the engine being well inside the tunnel some good work by driver, fireman, and train crew allowed the train to be uncoupled behind and ahead of the burning coaches. The rear two coaches were manhandled away by the train crew and passengers, and the engine and eight coaches went ahead to Grantshouse to report the incident and to summon assistance.

Not long after reading the Ministry of Transport Report on the Penmanshiel fire I was travelling on an East Coast express when I smelt burning. On looking out I could see nothing, but as the smell grew stronger I looked out again and saw that the leading end of the coach I was riding in was well alight, with flames three to four feet long coming up between the leading coach (a BG full of magazines) and the brake end of my coach. The train was travelling at about 55mph and No 60503 *Lord President* was roaring away at the front end so, with the details of the Penmanshiel fire fresh in my mind, I pulled the communication cord and the train came to a stand on a four-track section of the main line. A colleague and I jumped out and whilst I ran to inform the driver of what was happening my colleague climbed into the leading van and threw out a couple of extinguishers. He jumped back on the track, I ran back from the engine and we got the fire well under control with the two extinguishers. The driver ran back with a bucket of water, the guard came up with another extinguisher and together we put out the flames, although there was still plenty of smouldering wood. A minute or two later a light engine came along the slow line and its fireman played his slaker pipe on the wood. Two or three minutes after this fire engines came charging across the fields on both sides of the line, but there was little for the firemen to do except to chop away the damaged woodwork and make sure everything was safe. Not long afterwards we were on our way again and at the next station the train stopped to report the occurence; to save time it was decided that the train could proceed with a porter travelling in the van to see that everything remained alright. Consequently the train, and those following, were not extensively delayed. The engine, No 60503, was a real fire-thrower; it appeared that a red-hot cinder had lodged in the vestibule sheeting and the ensuing flames had ignited the coach ends.

The greatest delay to main-line services was caused by the weather. The winter of 1946/7 was extremely severe, particularly in the early part of 1947, with heavy snowfalls, and although the main line was blocked at times this was only for a short period, whereas some of the branch lines were out of action for six weeks or more. When the snow started to melt it caused a large amount of flooding, particularly on the low ground around Selby and York, and main-line trains had to be diverted, at first via Selby Canal, Gascoigne Wood and Church Fenton, and later via Knottingley and Church Fenton. This flooding was comparatively static and it did not damage the railway tracks to any great extent, so that when the water eventually drained away and the track had dried out it was not long before train services could be restored.

However, it was a totally different story 18 months later when, on 12 August 1948, after six days of heavy rain just north of the Scottish border, small streams turned into raging torrents washing away everything in their path. In the period 6 to 8

August, 4.18in of rain fell on the area, and when a further 6.28in fell on 12 August the ensuing floods caused severe damage to the East Coast main line, particularly north of Berwick, where bridges were washed away, and slips, landslides, and washouts affected the line at several places. Near Ayton a culvert through an embankment collapsed, blocking the path of the water on its way down to the sea. Consequently the railway embankment acted as a dam, trapping thousands of gallons of water on its west side.

The main line was also blocked south of Berwick. So was the Carlisle-Edinburgh route, together with the Tweedmouth-Kelso-St Boswells branch, although not as severely as the line between Berwick and Dunbar.

The down non-stop 'Flying Scotsman' was halted north of Alnmouth because of the flood damage south of Berwick and it had to retrace its steps to Newcastle, travelling across to Carlisle to take the Waverley route to Edinburgh. However, the 10.5am Kings Cross to Edinburgh train headed by No 60529 *Pearl Diver* had preceded it but could get no further than Tynehead because of flooding and a landslide across the track. Consequently the 'Scotsman' had to return to Carlisle to set off again for Edinburgh, this time via the Caledonian route through Carstairs. It finally arrived at Edinburgh (West End) ten hours late at 3.51am; there the passengers were met by refreshment trolleys and a specially opened refreshment room.

The passengers on the 10.5am from Kings Cross stranded at Tynehead were a little more fortunate as a lorry-load of refreshments was sent out from Edinburgh for them. They were eventually collected by seven buses and transported to Edinburgh, where they arrived at 1.40am – only seven hours late.

In the days immediately following the disaster trains between London and Edinburgh continued to use the Newcastle-Carlisle-Carstairs route, although there were two exceptions: the 'Flying Scotsman' ran via Selby Canal, Gascoigne Wood, Leeds City, Skipton, and Carlisle, and thence via Carstairs to Edinburgh, whilst the 'Queen of Scots' Pullman ran direct from Carlisle to Glasgow, with a connection for Edinburgh passengers at Carstairs. Local services were run between Newcastle and Berwick, and Edinburgh and Dunbar, and buses provided a service to the stations on the closed section of line between Berwick and Dunbar. In addition a fleet of motor lorries was used to rescue merchandise from five freight trains isolated by the flood damage.

By 17 August it was possible to reopen the Waverley route and the Tweedmouth-Kelso line, whereupon the East Coast services were rerouted, running over the main line from Newcastle to Tweedmouth, along the Tweed valley, passing from former North Eastern to North British lines beyond Sprouston, thence via Kelso, St. Boswells, Galashiels and Portobello, where the main line was rejoined for the short run into Edinburgh Waverley. Trains using this route were leaving Kings Cross and Edinburgh on time but were expected to be about one to two hours late at the other end.

The next move was the introduction of a temporary timetable on 23 August, with trains being allowed an extra 90 minutes for the overall journey via Kelso. As summer running was still in force the 'Flying Scotsman' was still in the period of non-stop working, but because of the diversion time was allowed for a water stop at Tweedmouth or Galashiels, and for taking banking assistance from Hardengreen on the up journey.

The enthusiastic Haymarket drivers thought that the journey could be made non-stop in spite of the extra 15 miles involved, so spurning the banking assistance and the water stop they proceeded to run through from Edinburgh to Lucker water troughs, and thence non-stop to Kings Cross. It was also found possible to perform the same non-stop running in the opposite direction, the water picked up at Lucker lasting the engines through to Edinburgh. Altogether this feat was performed seventeen times – nine times in the up direction and eight in the down – by three Haymarket drivers, McLeod, Stevenson, and Swan, before the summer timetable ended.

A second emergency timetable was introduced on 6 September 1948, with trains from Kings Cross and Edinburgh starting earlier. For instance the 7.30pm Kings Cross to Aberdeen was retimed to depart at 6.45pm, and the 1.45pm Edinburgh to Kings Cross at 1.0pm. This practice was continued in a special supplement to the winter timetable which came into force on 27 September.

North of Berwick work was soon put in hand to repair the flood damage. The embankment near Ayton was cut away to allow a controlled dispersal of the floodwater; landslides were cleared from the line; slips were filled and held by retaining walls; and work commenced on erecting temporary bridges. In fact work went ahead so well that it was possible to reopen the Berwick-Dunbar section to freight traffic on 25 October 1948, and to passenger traffic on 1 November. Needless to say severe speed restrictions were necessary over the temporary bridges, and at many other points where the formation had been disturbed or destroyed.

Above: Class A4 4-6-2 No. 60034 *Lord Faringdon* passing through York station on the London-Edinburgh non-stop 'Flying Scotsman' on 12 June 1948. This was the only post-war year when the train ran non-stop./*W. Rogerson*

Below: Class A3 4-6-2 No. 60045 *Lemberg* in dark blue livery passing Beningbrough./*C. Ord*

Above right: Class J39 0-6-0 No. 4791 passing Eryholme on an up goods on 2 August 1947./*W. Rogerson*

Right: Class 8F 2-8-0 No. 3536 passing Croft Spa on an up goods on 28 June 1947. Note the previous number, 3136, on the smokebox door numberplate./*W. Rogerson*

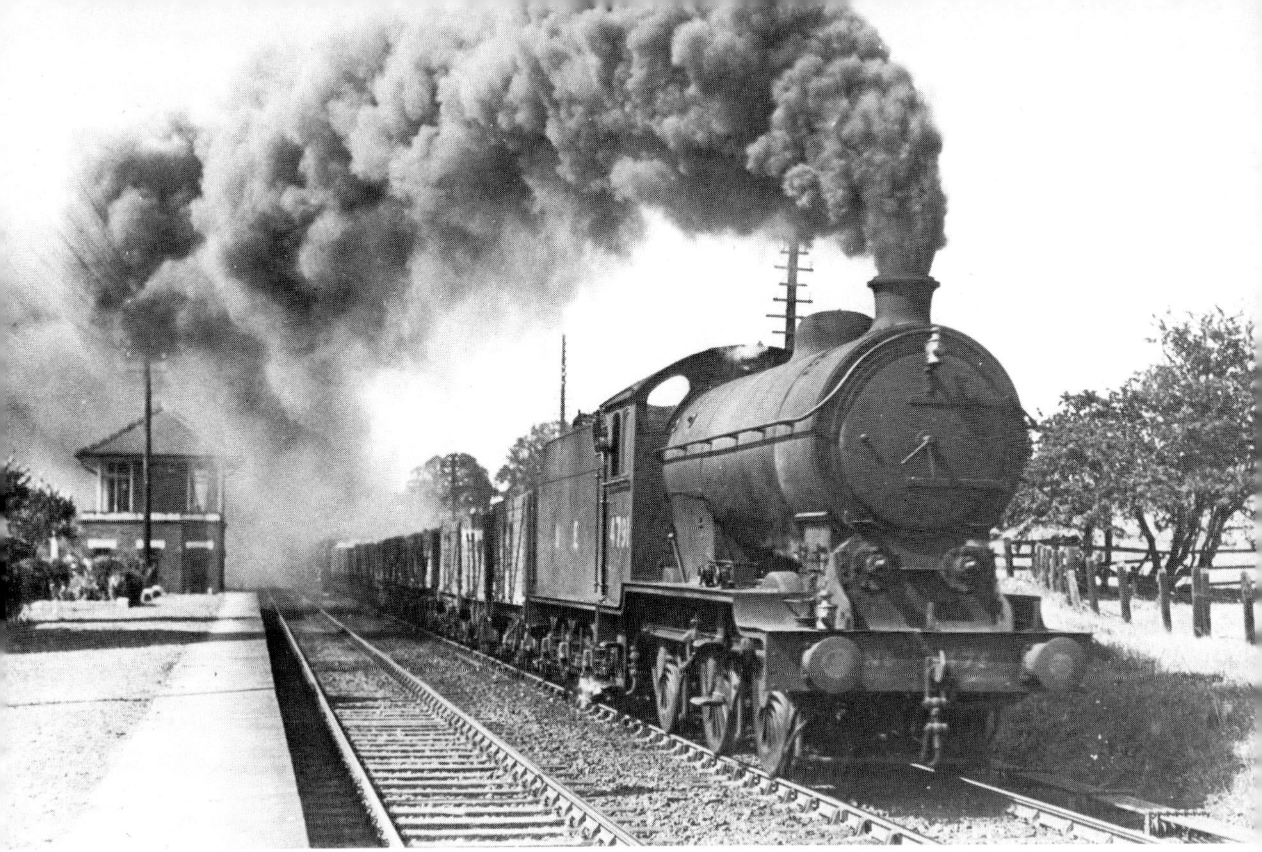

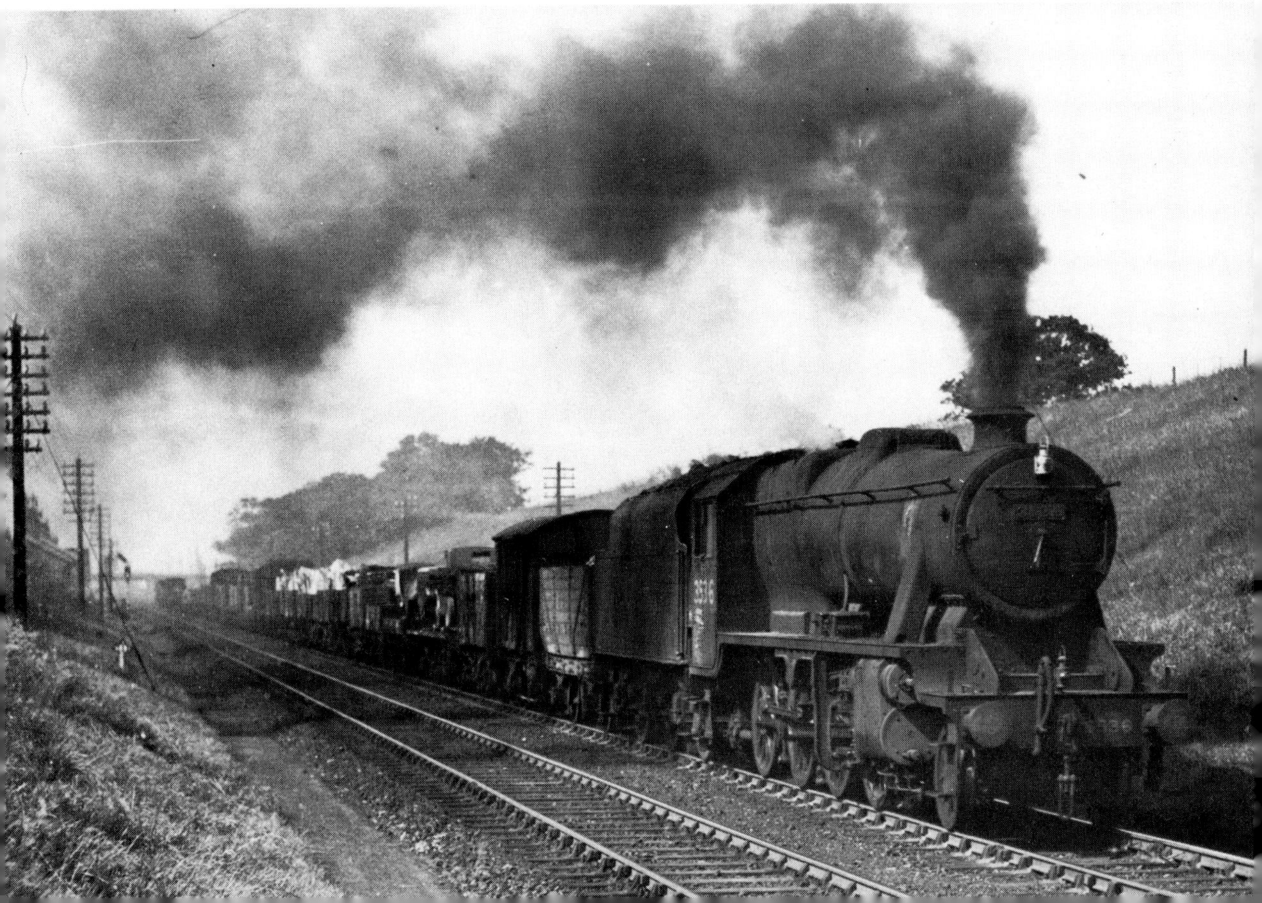

Above left: Class B1 4-6-0 No. 61071 leaving York.
/*Real Photos Ltd*

Left: A B16/2 (Gresley rebuild) 4-6-0 leaving York for Doncaster on an up goods./*BR*

Above: Class A3 4-6-2 No. 66 *Merry Hampton* derailed at Goswick on 26 October 1947./*Author's Collection*

Right: A winter view of the east end of Newcastle Central Station taken from the keep of the old Castle./*BR*

1950-1954

Unfortunately locomotive working on the main line deteriorated badly in June 1950. In that month the number of through engine workings between London and Newcastle was increased and Grantham, which had powered many northbound trains and worked them as far as Newcastle, was reduced to supplying only the crews. For some years Grantham engines had appeared at Newcastle with great regularity and some engines could be seen on the same trains for weeks on end, indicating good condition. With the re-introduction of London-Newcastle workings the picture changed; as failures increased, it was a case of providing any suitable engine that was available for East Coast expresses.

When the winter timetable came into force from 10 September 1951 the drive for longer engine workings was abandoned and engines were re-diagrammed for shorter journeys, enabling a locomotive to return to its home shed after almost every trip. Certainly mileage was reduced, but there was a compensatory saving in expense on repairs and failures – and what is often forgotten, a more reliable service to the customer, the passenger who pays the fare. Thus some 26 through workings per day were reduced to four – the up and down 'Tees-Tyne Pullman' worked by Kings Cross engines and men, and the up and down 'Night Scotsman', worked by Gateshead engines and men. This pattern of working remained almost unchanged until the introduction of diesel locomotives.

However, before the diesel locomotives appeared there came the diesel railcars, introduced in the North Eastern Region in June 1954, when they commenced running between Bradford, Leeds, and Harrogate. As 1954 was, therefore, the year in which steam supremacy was challenged, details are given of the main-line workings handled by the various sheds at that period. The data quoted are for July and August, for regular trains which ran Mondays to Fridays, although in one or two cases the workings were on three days a week, namely those in connection with the steamship services from Tyne Commission Quay. The details have been simplified as far as possible and do not include light engine movements between shed and station, nor empty stock workings between carriage sidings and station. It also must be stressed that these workings apply only to the locomotives and not to the men. For instance, a Gateshead engine working through to Grantham would probably have Gateshead men from Newcastle to York, York men on to Grantham, Grantham men back to York, and Heaton men from York to Newcastle. Because it was possible to refuel the crew far more quickly than the engine the crew usually started their return journey within an hour or two of their arrival, whereas an engine may not return for six or eight hours after requiring coaling, watering, turning, inspecting, and preparing.

Main Line Engine Diagrams Summer 1954
GATESHEAD
Two A1 engines
1.20am Newcastle-Kings Cross ('Night Scotsman')
10.15pm Kings Cross-Newcastle ('Night Scotsman')
11.21am Newcastle-Edinburgh ('North Briton')
5.14pm Edinburgh-Newcastle ('North Briton')
(*Note:* One engine worked the first part of the diagram on Mondays, Wednesdays and Fridays, and the second part of the diagram on Tuesdays, Thursdays and Saturdays. The other engine worked the first part on Tuesdays, Thursdays and Saturdays, and the second part on Mondays, Wednesdays and Fridays).
A1 engine
4.16am Newcastle-Edinburgh (10.35pm ex-Kings Cross)
10.00am Edinburgh-Newcastle ('Flying Scotsman')
7.5pm Newcastle-York (Bristol mail)
11.00pm York-Newcastle ('Aberdonian')
A1 engine
2.20am Newcastle-Edinburgh (Parcels)
10.27am Edinburgh-Newcastle
A3 engine
6.45am Newcastle-Edinburgh (12.55am ex-Kings Cross)
2.30pm Edinburgh-Newcastle
A1 engine
11.20pm Newcastle-York (8.00pm ex-Edinburgh)
6.40am York-Edinburgh
4.35pm Edinburgh-Newcastle (Fish)
A2 engine
11.50am Newcastle-Edinburgh (Parcels)
5.35pm Edinburgh-York (Fish)
1.35am York-Newcastle (Parcels)
A3 engine
12.20pm Newcastle-Edinburgh (10.5am ex-York)
11.30pm Edinburgh-Newcastle
A3 engine
7.40pm Newcastle-Edinburgh

3.10am Duddingston-Heaton (Goods)
A3 engine
2.35pm Newcastle-York-Leeds
7.20pm Leeds-York-Newcastle
A2 engine
7.54pm Newcastle-Grantham (Goods)
2.13am Grantham-Newcastle ('The Tynesider')
A4 engine
2.34am Newcastle-Peterborough (9.35pm ex-Glasgow)
11.40am Peterborough-Newcastle (10.5am ex-Kings Cross)
A4 engine
12.30pm Newcastle-Grantham ('Flying Scotsman')
7.44pm Grantham-Newcastle (5.35pm ex-Kings Cross)
A4 engine
4.35pm Newcastle-Grantham ('Heart of Midlothian')
1.14am Grantham-Newcastle (10.45pm ex-Kings Cross)
V2 engine
7.50pm Forth-York (Goods)
12.55am York-Newcastle (Parcels)
A3 engine
12.7pm Newcastle-York (Via coast)
5.00pm York-Newcastle (Parcels)
V2 engine
3.10pm Newcastle-Darlington (Parcels)
7.50pm Darlington-Newcastle
3.25am Newcastle-York (Parcels)
9.30am York-Newcastle (Parcels)
A2 engine
9.35am Delaval-York (Stock)
4.0pm York-Doncaster (Stock)
5.45pm Doncaster-Westwood (Stock)
2.28am Peterborough-Newcastle (12.55am ex-Kings Cross)
V2 engine
10.6pm Newcastle-York (Parcels)
1.55am York-Gateshead (Goods)
A1 engine MWFO
9.18am Newcastle-York
12.38pm York-Newcastle (9.5am ex-Kings Cross)
A3 engine
8.27pm Newcastle-York (Parcels)
2.25am York-Newcastle (Bristol mail)
A3 engine MWFO
12.53pm Newcastle-York (8.35am ex-Glasgow)
(Return on C750 Fruit or as required)

In addition a Class A1 engine was provided continuously for emergency purposes.
    Thus Gateshead shed had to provide daily for 23 diagrams calling for A1, A2, A3, A4 or V2 engines,

but although a specific type of engine was specified for each diagram this was not always supplied in practice, when measures had to be taken to cover the failure of an engine, or the non-arrival of an engine to take up the second part of its diagram. There were additional diagrams on Fridays and Saturdays: in the summer of 1954 the former called for five Pacifics and three V2s, and on the Saturday for seven Pacifics and eight V2s. With the help of B1 4-6-0 engines the peak summer Saturday diagrams called for 47 engines, excluding special trains, excursions etc, the power for which was arranged on a 'one-off' basis and could not, of course, be prepared months in advance as happened with the regular diagrams.

HEATON
A1 engine
5.47am Heaton Carriage Sdgs-Sunderland (Empty)
7.53am Sunderland-Grantham
2.26pm Grantham-Newcastle ('Northumbrian')
A3 engine
7.15am Heaton-York (Goods)
3.2pm York-Newcastle (8.45am ex-Bristol)
A1 engine
12.37pm Newcastle-York (To Bristol)
4.20pm York-Newcastle (Via Coast. Ex-Bristol)
10.30pm Newcastle-York (Via Coast)
3.50am York-Newcastle (Via Coast)
A3 engine
9.55am Newcastle-York-Leeds (Via Coast. To Liverpool)
4.35pm Leeds-Harrogate-Newcastle (Ex-Liverpool)
A3 engine
11.5am Newcastle-York-Leeds
5.00pm Leeds-York-Newcastle (Via Coast)
A3 engine
7.25pm Newcastle-York
12.25am York-Newcastle (Parcels)
A3 engine
5.32pm Newcastle-York
10.5pm York-Newcastle (Parcels)
A1 engine
8.15am Newcastle-York (To Bristol)
11.30am York Yard-Heaton (Goods)
5.40pm Newcastle-Edinburgh ('Queen of Scots')
10.40pm Edinburgh-Newcastle ('Night Scotsman')
A2 engine
6.58am Newcastle-York
11.30am York-Newcastle (8.2am ex-Birmingham)
4.18pm Newcastle-Edinburgh (Men change at Tweedmouth)
11.53pm Edinburgh-Newcastle (Parcels)

Heaton provided two A3 and four V2 for regular Saturday workings.

YORK
A1 engine
9.56pm York-Kings Cross (7.25pm ex-Newcastle)
7.55am Kings Cross-York
A1 engine
7.37pm York-Newcastle (11.16am ex-Bristol)
1.54am Newcastle-York (7.35pm ex-Aberdeen)
V2 engine
11.15pm York-Newcastle (7.15pm ex-Kings Cross)
8.37am Newcastle-York (To Bournemouth)
V2 engine
1.56pm York-Newcastle (Via Coast, Ex-Liverpool)
10.30pm Heaton Up Yard-York (Goods)
V2 engine
8.35am York-Newcastle
1.24pm Newcastle-York (Parcels)
9.30pm York-Sheffield Mid (Bristol Mail)
12.55am Sheffield Mid-York (Bristol Mail)
A2 engine
10.5am York-Newcastle
3.57pm Newcastle-York (To Birmingham)
11.10pm Dringhouses-Newcastle (Goods)
3.15am Heaton Up Yd.-York Up Yd. (Goods)
A2 engine
5.10pm York-Darlington
7.17pm Darlington-York (Parcels)
12.3am York-Grantham (Parcels)
7.33am Grantham-York (Parcels)
A2 engine
1.9am York-Newcastle (8.20pm ex-Kings Cross)
5.35am Heaton Up Yard-Dringhouses (Goods)
1.40pm York-Newcastle (7.20am ex-Colchester)
5.30pm Park Lane-Dringhouses (Goods)
V2 engine
10.0am York-Sheffield Mid (Newcastle-Bristol)
2.53pm Sheffield Mid.-York (Bristol-Newcastle)
9.35pm York-West Hartlepool
11.50pm West Hartlepool-Stockton (Light eng. & guard)
2.25am Stockton-York (Goods)

Separate diagrams were issued for Freight Locomotive & Trainmen's Working. At York, for example, these called for 18 V2s, four B16/3s, 27 B16s and two B1s (for the Brunswick working). However, not all of these ran every day. For the York District alone this required a volume of 98 pages, to list all the workings in detail. The Main Line Passenger Engine Working Book from which details are quoted above ran to 72 pages, but this covered all North Eastern Region sheds working Main Line trains, and also those trains worked by crews from the Eastern and Scottish Regions.

HAYMARKET
Pacific engine
10.10am Edinburgh-Newcastle
3.6pm Newcastle-Edinburgh ('Flying Scotsman')
10.20pm Edinburgh-Newcastle
2.42am Newcastle-Edinburgh (Ex-Colchester)
Pacific engine
12.00noon Edinburgh-Newcastle ('Queen of Scots')
3.36pm Newcastle-Edinburgh (10.5am ex-Kings Cross)
11.20pm Edinburgh-Newcastle (To Colchester)
3.35am Newcastle-Edinburgh ('Night Scotsman')
Pacific engine
2.0pm Edinburgh-Newcastle ('Heart of Midlothian')
7.23pm Newcastle-Edinburgh ('Heart of Midlothian')
Pacific engine
7.20pm Edinburgh-Newcastle (Parcels)
12.38am Newcastle-Edinburgh ('Aberdonian')
Pacific engine
11.0pm Edinburgh-Newcastle ('Aberdonian')
3.4am Newcastle-Edinburgh (8.20pm ex–Kings Cross)
Pacific engine
8.0pm Edinburgh-Newcastle
12.53am Newcastle-Edinburgh (7.15pm ex-Kings Cross)
Class 8P engine MWFO
9.45am Edinburgh-Kings Cross ('Elizabethan')
Class 8P engine TThSO
9.30am Kings Cross-Edinburgh ('Elizabethan')

The sight of the rebuilt P2 engines at work south of Newcastle always seemed odd, just as it did when old favourites *Merry Hampton*, *Knight of Thistle*, and *Ladas* started appearing at Newcastle from the south instead of the north. This was in the summer of 1950 when *Tagalie* (formerly *William Whitelaw*) and *Merry Hampton* moved from Haymarket to Doncaster, and *Knight of Thistle* and *Ladas* from Haymarket to Kings Cross in exchange for A3 Nos 90, 96, 97, and 98. On journeys to Scotland in the 1930s and 1940s Edinburgh seemed so close when one of these engines backed on at Newcastle, although the border was 70 miles away and Edinburgh was 124. Except for the use of Nos 2563 *William Whitelaw* and 2564 *Knight of Thistle* on the non-stop 'Flying Scotsman' in the 1920s, and their occasional use on specials for some important football or rugby matches in London, the Scottish Pacifics did not normally work south of Newcastle.

The 'Scarborough Flyer' was re-introduced on 5 June 1950 but it ran only on Fridays, Saturdays and

Sundays in the down direction, and on Mondays, Saturdays and Sundays in the up. It never attained its pre-war eminence.

May 1951 saw the completion at York of the colour-light signalling installation, on which work had started prior to the war. This brought about the closure of Chaloners Whin, South Points, Locomotive Yard, Platform, Leeman Road, Waterworks, and Clifton manual boxes, and greatly speeded up the operation of the station. Locomotive Yard box, dating from 1909, was the largest manually-operated box in the country, with 295 levers.

The name of the box puzzled me when I first got to know York station in my schooldays: the main engine shed at Clifton was north of the station, whereas Locomotive Yard was south. However, I later discovered that even prior to the opening of the present station in 1877 the locomotive sheds had been in the vicinity of Locomotive Yard box and, in fact, the South shed buildings remained until the 1960s.

The first BR Pacific No 70000 *Britannia* was turned out of Crewe Works in January 1951 and it was on display at a Railway Exhibition at York in connection with the Festival of Britain in June 1951. For this event it worked to and from York on ordinary trains and fortunately Cecil Ord was able to capture it with his camera when it returned south on 18 June 1951, heading the 1.52pm York to Kings Cross train.

Another event connected with the Festival of Britain was the naming of the up and down afternoon service between London and Edinburgh, which became 'The Heart of Midlothian' from 7 May 1951. Also named was the 10.35pm Newcastle-Kings Cross sleeper, and the opposite working at 11.45pm from Kings Cross, which from 5 June 1950 became 'The Tynesider'. At the same time the summer Kings Cross-Tyne Commission Quay service in connection with the Bergen Steamship Company's vessels was christened 'The Norseman'; as this ran on Wednesdays and Saturdays only (also certain Thursdays in July and August) the actual date of introduction was 7 June 1950.

To commemorate the Coronation of Queen Elizabeth II the non-stop working between London and Edinburgh was renamed 'The Elizabethan' when it started its summer season on 29 June 1953. Compared with the running of 'The Capitals Limited' in the previous summer it was accelerated by 21min in the down direction (Kings Cross dep 9.35am Edinburgh arr 4.20pm), although the through coaches to Aberdeen arrived only two minutes earlier. In the up direction the

acceleration was 22min (Edinburgh dep 9.45am Kings Cross arr 4.30pm). Here again the Aberdeen passengers did not benefit as their departure time (5.50am) remained the same.

Thus the time in each direction between London and Edinburgh was down to 6hr 45min – 15min faster than the 1939 non-stop 'Scotsman', although the trains in 1939 and 1953 were worked by the same class of locomotive, namely the Gresley A4 streamlined Pacifics. The first of these appeared in 1935 and some were therefore 18 years old, but they were going better than ever. However, in 1954 the timings were reduced yet again, to 6½hr in both directions – and still the trains were worked by A4 engines!

Strangers on the main line north of York in the 1950s were LM Class 5, BR Class 5 and 'Jubilee' 4-6-0s on excursions from south Yorkshire and the Midlands to Tyneside. However, the most surprising events occurred on 29 and 30 October 1954 when severe flooding in Scotland disrupted West Coast and Midland line traffic. Diverted via Berwick, Newcastle, York and Leeds were such trains as the up and down 'Thames-Clyde' (Glasgow St. Enoch to London St. Pancras); the up 'Royal Scot' (10.0am Glasgow Central to Euston); and the up 'Mid-day Scot' (1.30pm Glasgow Central to Euston). 'Royal Scot' No 46108 actually worked through from Glasgow to Leeds via this unusual route on the up 'Thames-Clyde' on 30 October, and numerous LMS Pacifics were observed between Edinburgh and Newcastle on both passenger and freight trains: for instance, on 30 October the up 'Royal Scot' arrived at Newcastle behind 4-6-2 No 46221 *Queen Elizabeth*, but there the stranger was replaced by V2 No 60981 as the LMS Pacifics were not allowed to work into Leeds.

A most spectacular derailment occurred between York and Thirsk on 5 June 1950 when the heat of the sun buckled the rails of the up main line just south of Tollerton. This was because the fishplates had not been oiled sufficiently and the rails were not free to expand. Although the track looked all right to the driver of the up 'Flying Scotsman' his train released the rails from tension and its rear end lurched so violently that the solebars of the tail-end van were seriously distorted. The guard stopped the train but all he could locate was a broken dynamo belt and he thought that this must have caught something on the track. Consequently, after a few minutes he allowed the train to proceed to York. But he asked a passing platelayer if he would tell York that the train would be stopping for examination, and also mentioned to the platelayer the lurch that had been experienced. The platelayer cycled off to have a look at the track a couple of miles up the line – only to find that the following train had already been derailed.

The 12.15pm from Newcastle was following the 'Scotsman' and after being checked at Alne it was allowed to continue on the main rather than being turned on to the slow line. On getting the road the driver accelerated to about 45mph, when he saw that the track ahead of him was severely buckled. It was impossible to stop in time and the engine, A1 No 60153 *Flamboyant*, was derailed to the left, ploughing across the up slow line and coming to rest leaning at about 45deg. on the cutting side. The first three coaches were also derailed, with the leading pair spread out across all four tracks. Fortunately no other train was involved and no one was seriously hurt.

On 28 October 1953 the third serious accident occurred at Goswick, again concerning the turnout involved in the 1907 and 1947 accidents. On this occasion the derailment was due to part of the engine's valve gear becoming detached and catching the stretcher bar of the points. This opened the left-hand switch rail and caused the engine – A2/1 No 60509 *Waverley* – to be derailed with all the nine vehicles of its train, the 9.15pm Glasgow to Colchester. Only one of the 58 passengers required first-aid treatment.

Some weeks later, on 17 December 1953, the 12.41am up parcels train from Edinburgh, headed by A2 No 60530, struck a length of pre-fabricated Decauville track which had fallen on to the up main line from a goods train passing Longniddry Junction. The engine suffered badly; it was parted from its tender, thrown over the up platform and finally came to rest, wheels uppermost, at the bottom of the embankment, having turned through 180deg. The tender remained upright between the tracks about 40yds ahead of the engine, but it too had been turned round. The leading six vans were demolished and many of the others were derailed and buffer-locked. The fireman was killed and the driver received serious injuries.

The final serious accident of the period in this section occurred in the North Eastern Region where, on 20 January 1954, the 2.0pm Kings Cross Edinburgh express – the 'Heart of Midlothian' – was derailed at Thirsk due to faults in the cabling to two sets of electrically-operated points, and to rain-soaked ground. As the express was approaching the signalman operated points connected with a movement on the up line, and the current from these partially operated a pair of facing points in the down main on which the express was running at 70-75mph! Fortunately as the points opened the signals guarding them automatically went to danger. The driver braked hard when he saw what had been a green colour-light turn to a single yellow, and the next signal from green to red. He was unable to stop at the red signal at the north end of Thirsk station platform and the train was derailed at the points 187yds ahead of the signal and right under the eyes of the signalman, who was powerless to avert the derailment. Fortunately by the time the engine reached the points the speed was down to about 20mph and was still decreasing. Although the engine and the first four coaches were derailed the accident could have been much worse if the points had opened a few seconds later with the train travelling at high speed.

Above right: Class A1 4-6-2 No. 60142 *Edward Fletcher* leaving Edinburgh Waverley on the up 'Flying Scotsman'./*Author's Collection*

Right: Class A2 4-6-2 No. 60526 *Sugar Palm* heads a Newcastle-Liverpool express near York on July 24, 1950./*C. Ord*

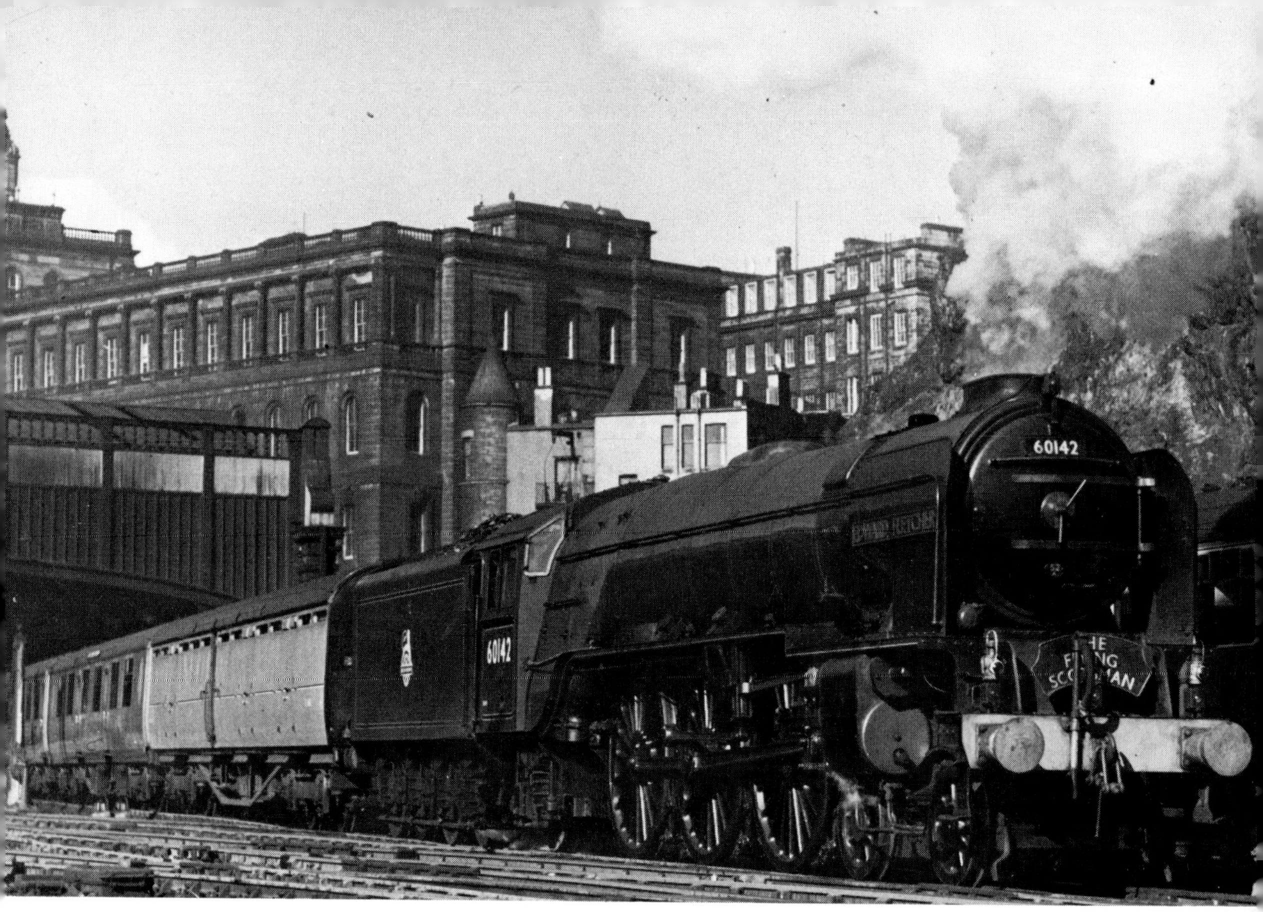
60142
60142

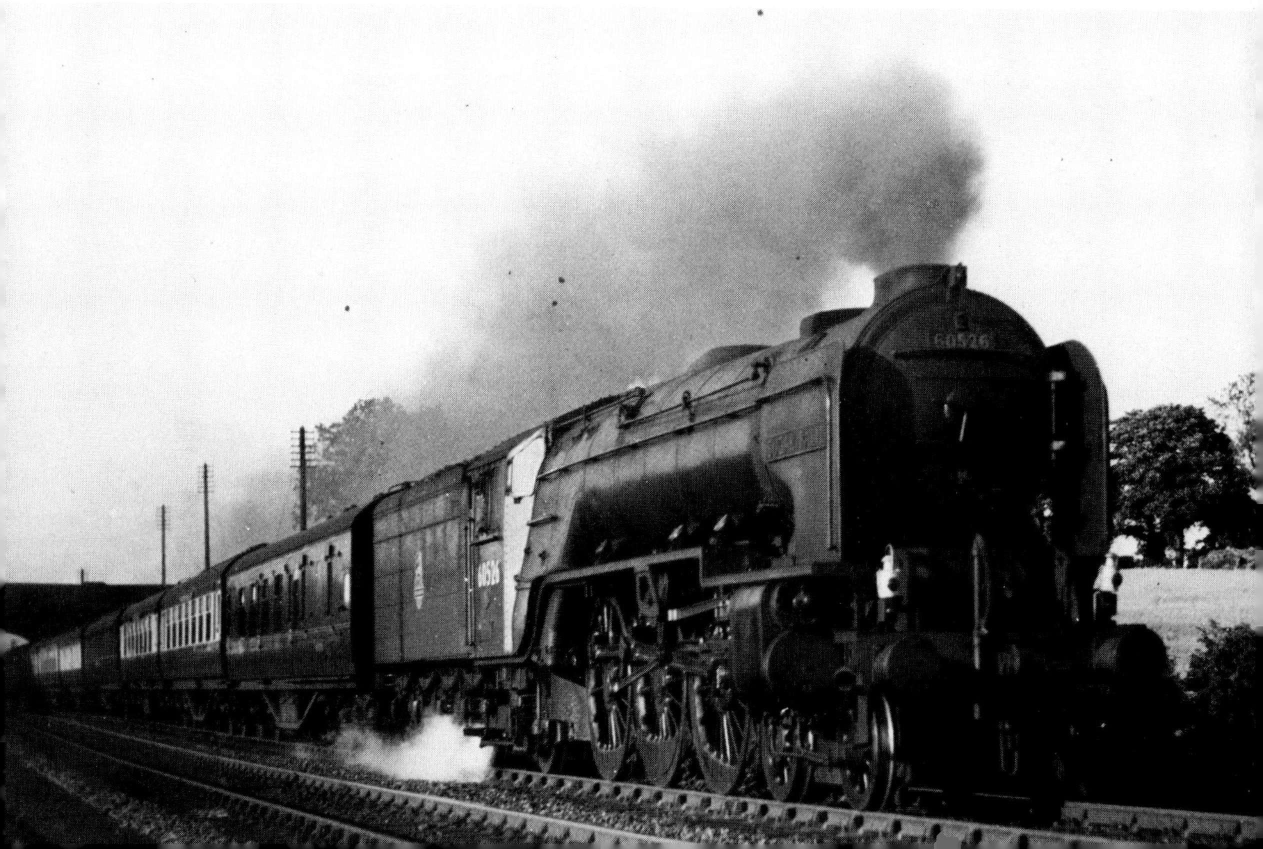

Top: King Edward Bridge over the Tyne, 2 September 1952./*BR*

Above: Signal gantry at the west end of Newcastle Central on 21 February 1951./*BR*

Above right: The original type of BR railcar introduced on the North Eastern Region./*BR*

Right: Pacific No. 70000 *Britannia* leaving York after being on show at a Festival of Britain exhibition on 18 June 1951./*C. Ord*

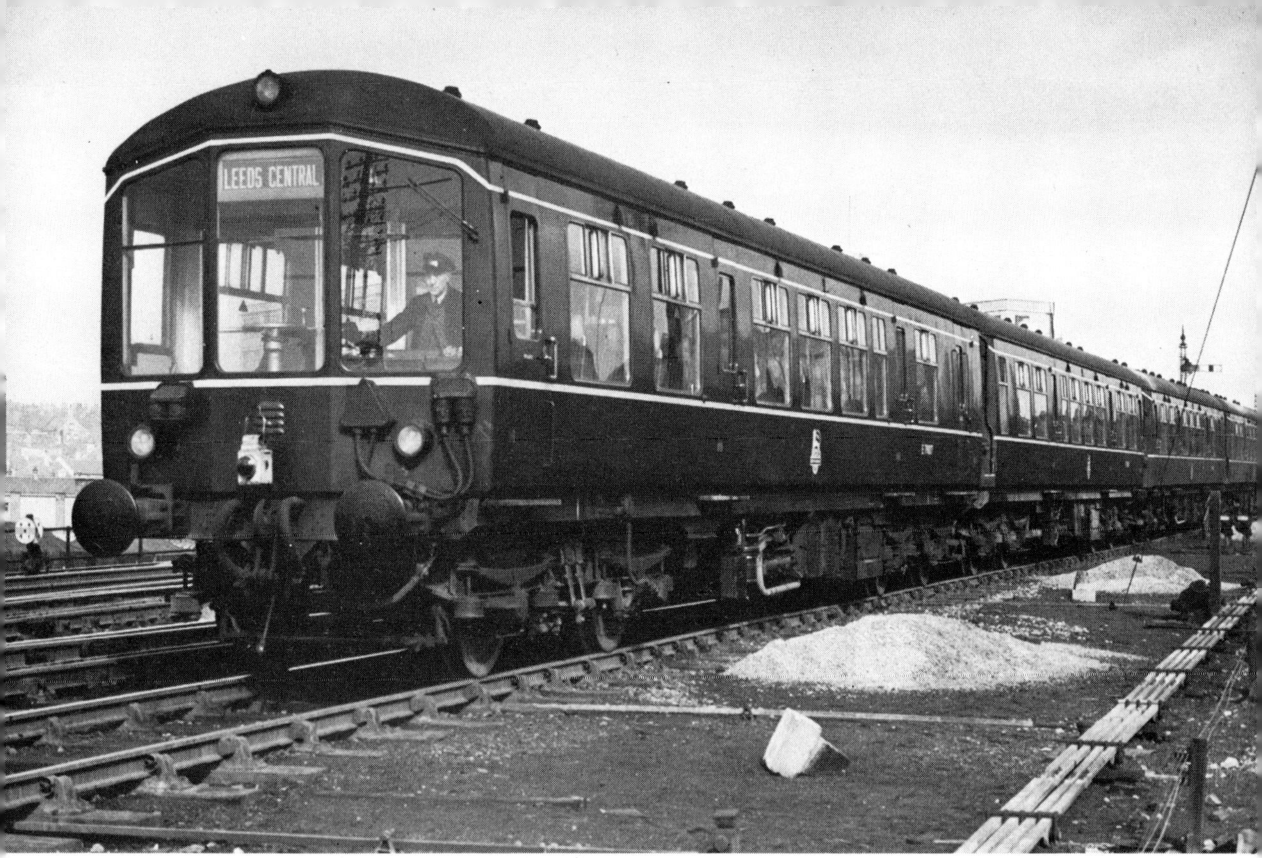
LEEDS CENTRAL

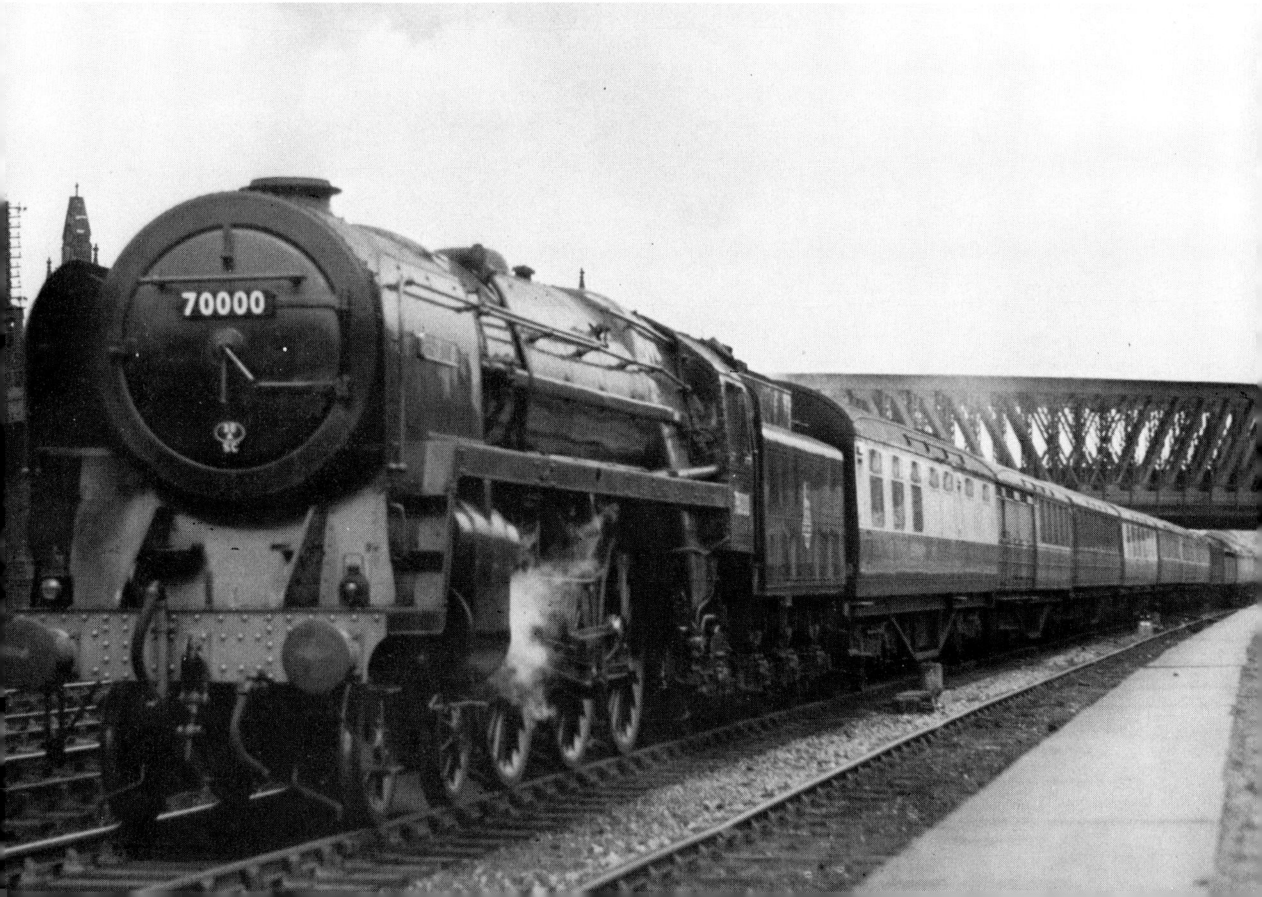
70000

1955-1959

The year 1957 saw the delivery of the first of the many main-line diesel electric locomotives ordered by British Railways. This was No D5500 from Brush, allocated to Stratford on 31 October. The first to be seen in the north-east was No D5510, which worked a special train to Thornaby for the formal opening of the new Motive Power Depot on 3 June 1958.

In March 1958 delivery commenced of the English Electric 2,000hp locomotives. Although the first seven (D200-6) were at first allocated to Stratford one of this batch, No D201, was transferred to Hornsey on 25 April for testing and driver training duties on the main line, working mainly between Kings Cross and Grantham or Cambridge.

On 21 June 1958 No D201 ventured northwards when it worked the down 'Flying Scotsman', at that time booked non-stop from London to Newcastle (268 miles) in 301min. It returned on the 5.5pm from Newcastle which, in spite of stops at Darlington, York, Doncaster, Retford and Hitchin, was allowed exactly the same time as the non-stop down working. This, apart from the Armstrong Whitworth locomotive in the mid-1930s, was the first main-line diesel locomotive to be seen in action on the North Eastern section of the main line.

For the winter of 1958-9 diagrams were introduced for the initial batch of English Electric diesels, Nos D201 and D206-9 then stationed at Hornsey, and these took them to Newcastle on certain trains. However, crew training and failures led to many of their turns being worked by steam locomotives. The first of this type to be allocated to the North Eastern Region was No D237, which arrived at Gateshead on 20 October 1959; eventually Gateshead had an allocation of more than 30 of the class.

Clearance tests with the prototype 'Deltic' locomotive were carried out in the north-east in January 1959, and on a trial run from Kings Cross to Newcastle on 15 March 1959 Driver Bill Hoole, with a ten-coach train and the dynamometer car, succeeded in covering the 268 miles in 236min – four minutes faster than the pre-war 'Silver Jubilee'. The 'Deltic' was subsequently put into regular service on the East Coast main line, but working between Kings Cross and Doncaster only.

The introduction of diesel shunters made redundant many 0-6-0T and 0-6-2T shunting locomotives, and similarly when diesel railcars were available in large numbers numerous 0-4-4T, 2-6-2T, 2-6-4T, and 4-6-2T became surplus. As experience was gained with the railcars they were used on longer workings, displacing 4-4-0 and 4-6-0 tender engines. On the freight side medium-power diesel locomotives replaced J39 0-6-0 and K3 2-6-0 engines, and the second half of the 1950s saw the first withdrawals of established classes which, but for dieselisation, would have given many more years of service. In addition the period also saw the extinction of some classes which, at one time, had been the pride of the main line.

For instance, the last D20 4-4-0 – the famous NER Class R – was condemned on 20 November 1957 when No 62395 was withdrawn from Alnmouth, where it had spent its last days on the local service to Newcastle. And yet two months earlier the first D49 4-4-0, built 20 years after the D20, had also gone to the scrapheap. The D49s were made redundant by the influx of railcars, and the reduction in their sphere of usefulness is well illustrated by the fact that in the following year no fewer than 30 were withdrawn.

Another well-known NER class, which had performed good work for many years, was also broached in 1958, when B16 4-6-0 No 61474 was withdrawn from Selby on 21 January. This was one of the ten original B16s of 1919.

1959 saw the first J39 0-6-0 and K3 2-6-0 engines scrapped, and also the disappearance of the sole W1 4-6-4 No 60700: this was, of course, the one-time 'Hush-Hush' engine built at Darlington in 1929 with a water tube boiler supplied by Yarrow & Co. of Glasgow. After extended trials the engine was rebuilt with a normal locomotive type boiler in 1937. It was stationed in the North Eastern Area when running in its original condition, but after rebuilding it was based on the former Great Northern section, normally working between Doncaster and London, though it did occasionally reach Newcastle and Edinburgh.

The little Easingwold Railway, opened in 1891, was closed in December 1957; for all those years it had been possible to see from main line trains the Easingwold train tucked away at the short bay platform at the north end (up side) of Alne station. Between 1891 and 1903 the company owned *Easingwold*, a Hudswell Clarke 0-6-0ST, which in 1903 was replaced by a second Hudswell Clarke engine of very similar design lettered 'Easingwold Railway No 2.' However, in 1947 No 2 was found to be beyond repair and until closure the line was worked by a J71 or J72 0-6-0T hired from British

Railways; it was one of the latter class, 68698 (carrying the chalked name *Omega*) which worked the last train on 27 December 1957. The line ceased to carry passengers in November 1948.

The widening of the main line between Alne and Pilmoor in 1932/3 was confined to the down side and thus the Easingwold bay at Alne escaped alteration. However not long after closure a widening scheme for the up side from Pilmoor to Alne meant the demolition of the up platform at Alne, including the Easingwold bay. Since this widening, completed in June 1960, all that can be seen (if you are quick enough) as you dash past at 100mph are the hedges between which the line curved away eastwards towards Easingwold.

The most notable accident to report in this period is that which occurred at York on the morning of 4 August 1958, Bank Holiday Monday, when the 9.26am arrival from Sunderland ran at speed into the buffers of No 12 bay platform. The leading bogie of the engine, A3 No 60036 *Colombo*, was torn off by the concrete buffer stop and provided a ramp for the engine to ride up over the buffers. The leading driving wheels came to rest on the platform, and the front end of the engine was actually touching the tobacco kiosk built under the northern wing of the footbridge steps. Fortunately only 11 passengers were injured, but *Colombo* suffered considerable damage, particularly to the front end, although the bogie was sound enough for use to get the engine to the shed. The greatest damage was sustained by the leading driving wheel on the right-hand side, which had the wheel and tyre fractured, three spokes badly distorted, and a pronounced 'flat' extending for more than 2ft. No formal accident report was published, but the collision is reputed to have been caused by the driver misreading signals and thinking he was running into the down main (through) platform, whereas he was routed into the adjoining bay platform.

On 19 April 1955 a collision occured on 'the largest railway crossing in the world' at the east end of Newcastle station when 2-6-4T No 42073 arriving on a train from Middlesbrough ran into the side of V2 No 60968. The 2-6-4T was derailed and the V2 was pushed over on to its side, but no one was injured.

The superiority of the four double-chimney A4 Pacifics was well known but it was not until May 1957 that a start was made on fitting the other 30 of the class. The first to be converted was No 60017 *Silver Fox* – one of the orginal engines – and the last Nos 60009 and 60032, in November 1958. Before the task was completed a start was made in fitting the earlier Pacifics with double chimneys,

the first treated being No 60055 *Woolwinder* in June 1958, and the last No 60092 *Fairway* in November 1959.

Complaints regarding poor smoke and steam clearance led to the fitting of small wing deflectors on the smokebox top of the A3 engines, but more efficient clearance was obtained when German trough-type deflectors were applied to the sides of the smokebox; 55 A3s were fitted with these devices between October 1960 and January 1963. However, the speed with which diesels were taking over was too much for the A3s. The first to be withdrawn was No 60104 *Solario* in December 1959, only eight months after it had been fitted with a double chimney. This engine was not a very common sight in the North Eastern Area, and its early demise was due to the fact that it had a cracked frame: this did not, at that time, presage the extinction of the class, although that came soon enough because of rapid dieselisation. However, a class for which there was little hope was the Thompson rebuild of the Gresley 2-8-2 engines and Nos 60503 *Lord President* and 60505 *Thane of Fife* were withdrawn in November 1959.

When the first English Electric 2,000hp locomotives were allocated to Gateshead shed they had no definite duties, but where a diesel was available, and where the driver for the duty was trained for that type of diesel locomotive, then the new engine could be used. Thus some of the earliest workings (at the end of 1959) were:

	arr	dep	
Newcastle	–	4.36am	(11.20pm ex-Kings Cross)
Edinburgh	7.5am	10.0am	(Up 'Flying Scotsman')
Newcastle	12.15pm	2.51pm	(Down 'Flying Scotsman')
Edinburgh	5.2pm	7.12pm	(Parcels)
Newcastle	9.52pm	–	

This was in place of a Gateshead A1 Pacific. Also:

	arr	dep	
Newcastle	–	6.55am	
Edinburgh	9.46am	12.5pm	(Up 'Queen of Scots')
Newcastle	2.14pm	6.17pm	(Down 'Heart of Midlothian')
Edinburgh	8.46pm	11.5pm	
Newcastle	1.29am	–	

This replaced a Heaton A1. Each of these turns involved 498 miles per day exclusive of light engine running.

In 1960 the diagrams were gradually extended, until with the timetable for the winter of 1960/1 a Gateshead Type 4 diesel was rostered to work from Edinburgh to London and back before returning to its home shed, covering 786 miles in 24hr, but soon such duties were taken over by the 'Deltics', which entered regular service on 1 June 1961.

New named trains introduced in the 1950s included 'The Talisman', which first ran on 17 September 1956, with a timing of 6hr 40min for the London-Edinburgh journey. The trains left Kings Cross and Waverley simultaneously at 4.0pm and engines were changed at Newcastle in both directions. The down train was worked between Kings Cross and Newcastle by a Kings Cross engine and crew, returning the next day on the 8.0am (7.50am SO) from Newcastle. The up train was handled between Newcastle and London by Gateshead men who returned the next day on the 10.10am from Kings Cross. North of Newcastle the trains were worked by a Haymarket engine and crew as an out and home turn.

The departure time of 4.0pm was the same as that of the pre-war 'Coronation', but the time allowed in 1956 was 40min more. Needless to say the workings were generally entrusted to the reliable A4 Pacifics, although A1 Pacifics did appear occasionally.

With the introduction of the summer timetable on 17 June 1957 a morning 'Talisman' was inaugurated, leaving Kings Cross at 7.45am and Edinburgh at 7.30am and being allowed 6hr 45min in both directions: at the same time the afternoon 'Talisman' had five minutes added to its timing. Each set of coaches could now be used for a return journey each day.

In the next timetable, for the winter of 1957/8, another named train appeared, the 'Fair Maid', but this was only the morning 'Talisman' renamed and extended to Perth. In spite of British Rail's claim that the new timetable was 'more orderly, with better use of engines, coaches, and train crews' the extension to Perth limited the coaches to a run in one direction only each day! In addition to the usual six minutes' stop at Newcastle, a two minutes stop at Darlington was introduced, increasing the overall time to Edinburgh in the down direction by one minute to 6hr 46min. In the up direction the 6.40am start from Perth necessitated an 8.30am departure from Edinburgh, and a 6hr 50min journey time to Kings Cross.

The inaugural down 'Fair Maid' was worked by A4 No 60015 *Quicksilver* to Newcastle, where it was replaced by No 60027 *Merlin*, which had worked the corresponding up train. Between Newcastle and Kings Cross A1 No 60156 *Great Central* was in charge. The 'Fair Maid' lasted only a year: with the winter 1958/9 timetable the Perth extension was withdrawn and the morning service resumed the name 'Talisman', retaining the 8.30am departure from Edinburgh. From the same time the morning service stopped also at Berwick in both directions, but the afternoon trains stopped only at Newcastle.

Early in 1958 improvements were completed at Shaftholme Junction; a curve in the main line was eased to allow higher speed running – 100mph instead of 60mph – and at the same time a new signalbox was built, replacing the old Great Northern box which had stood there for many years. In pre-Grouping days, although the box was owned and staffed by the Great Northern, the whole of the expenses were borne by the North Eastern. This was due to the fact that the NER was treated as the 'later comer'. As the box had been opened for the North Eastern's convenience when the line from Selby was opened in 1871 it was liable for the costs. In 1902-4 the expenses amounted to about £300 a year, of which £200 was for signalmen's wages and the remainder for 'lamping', 'fogging', maintenance, and the supply of coal, oil, and stationery etc.

Above right: Class A1 4-6-2 No. 60125 *Scottish Union* passing York MPD on the down 'Flying Scotsman' on 17 July 1957 / K. Hoole

Right: Class A3 No. 60081 *Shotover* leaving Harrogate on the up 'Queen of Scots' Pullman./*Real Photos Ltd*

Top: The right-hand leading driving wheel of A3 No. 60036 *Colombo* after the buffer stop collision at York on 4 August 1958./*Author's Collection*

Above: The first diesel-hauled 'Flying Scotsman' north of York on 21 June 1958, headed by EE Type 4 No. D201./*C. Ord*

Above right: Class A2/3 No. 60523 *Sun Castle* at York on 20 August 1959./*K. Hoole*

Right: Class A1 No. 60128 *Bongrace* leaving York on a test run to Darlington on 1 May 1958./*K. Hoole*

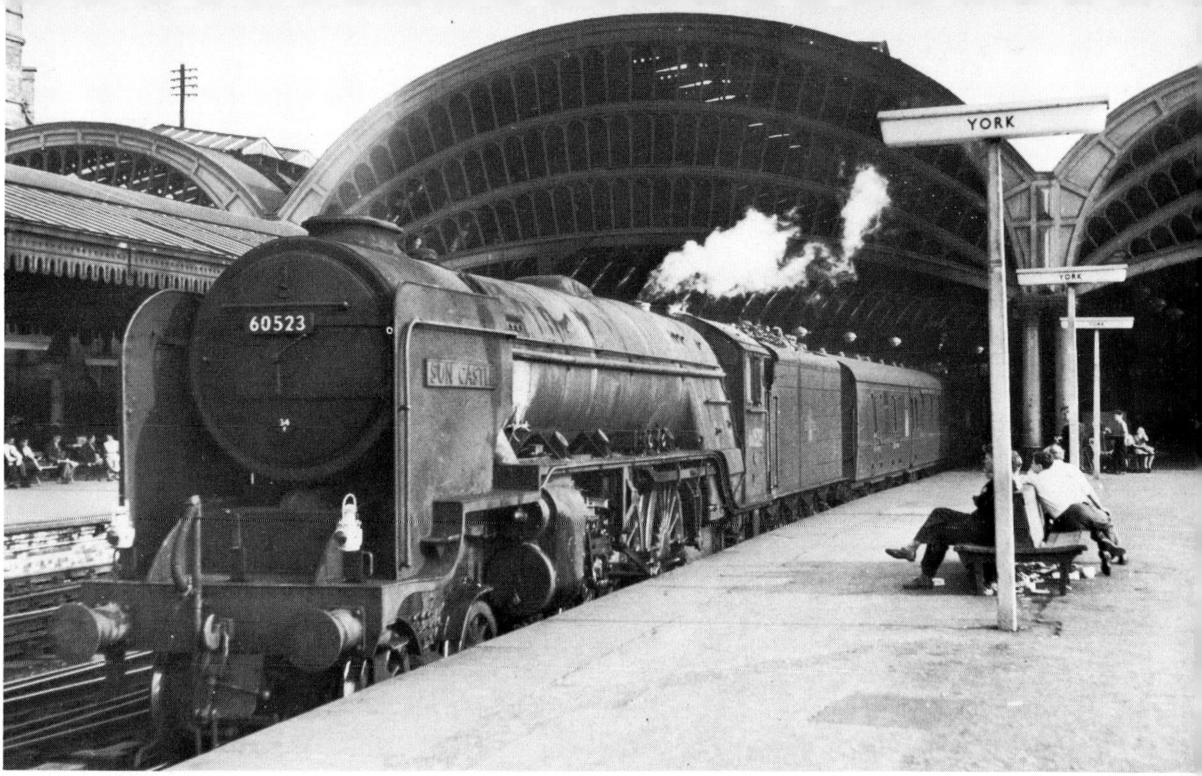
YORK
60523

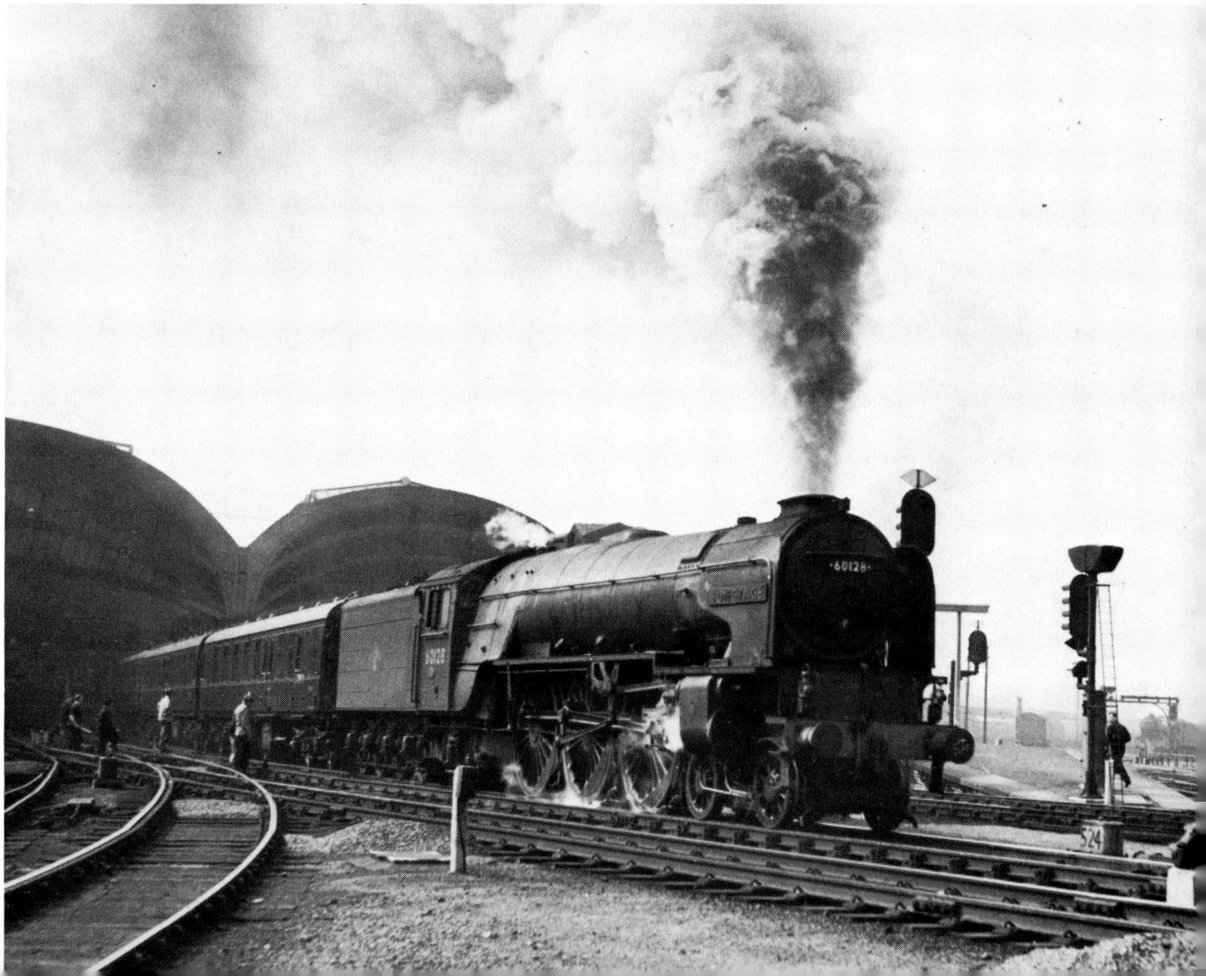
60128
524

Above: Class D49 4-4-0 No. 62740 *The Bedale* leaving Harrogate on the 'Harrogate Sunday Pullman.'/*Author's Collection*

Left: LM 'Jubilee' 4-6-0 No. 45618 *New Hebrides* entering Bishop Auckland on a diverted Chesterfield to Newcastle excursion./*Ian S. Carr*

Above right: Metro-Cammell railcar used in the Newcastle area. /*BR*

Right: Class V2 2-6-2 No. 60847 *St. Peter's School, York, A.D. 627* passing through York station on the up main line./*Ian S. Carr*

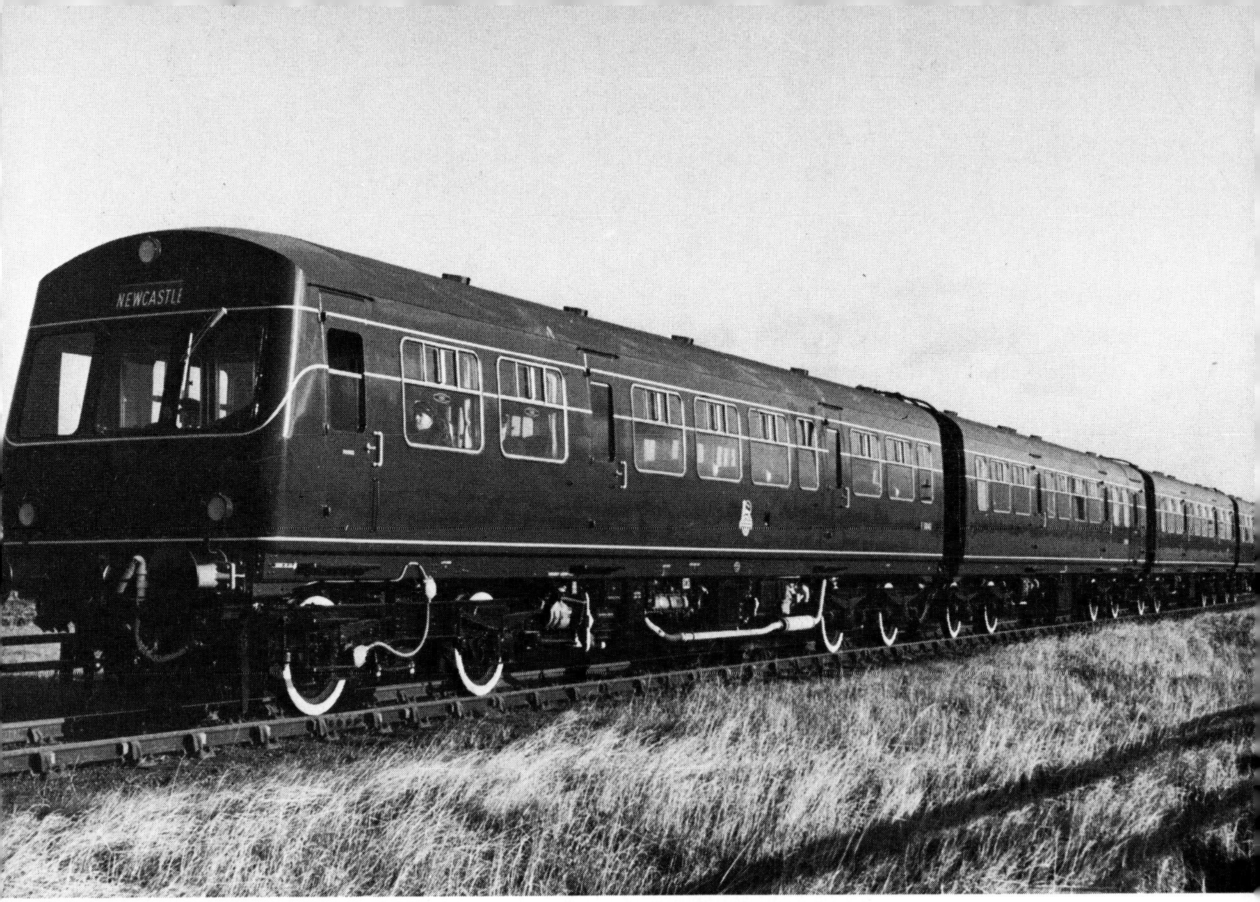
NEWCASTLE

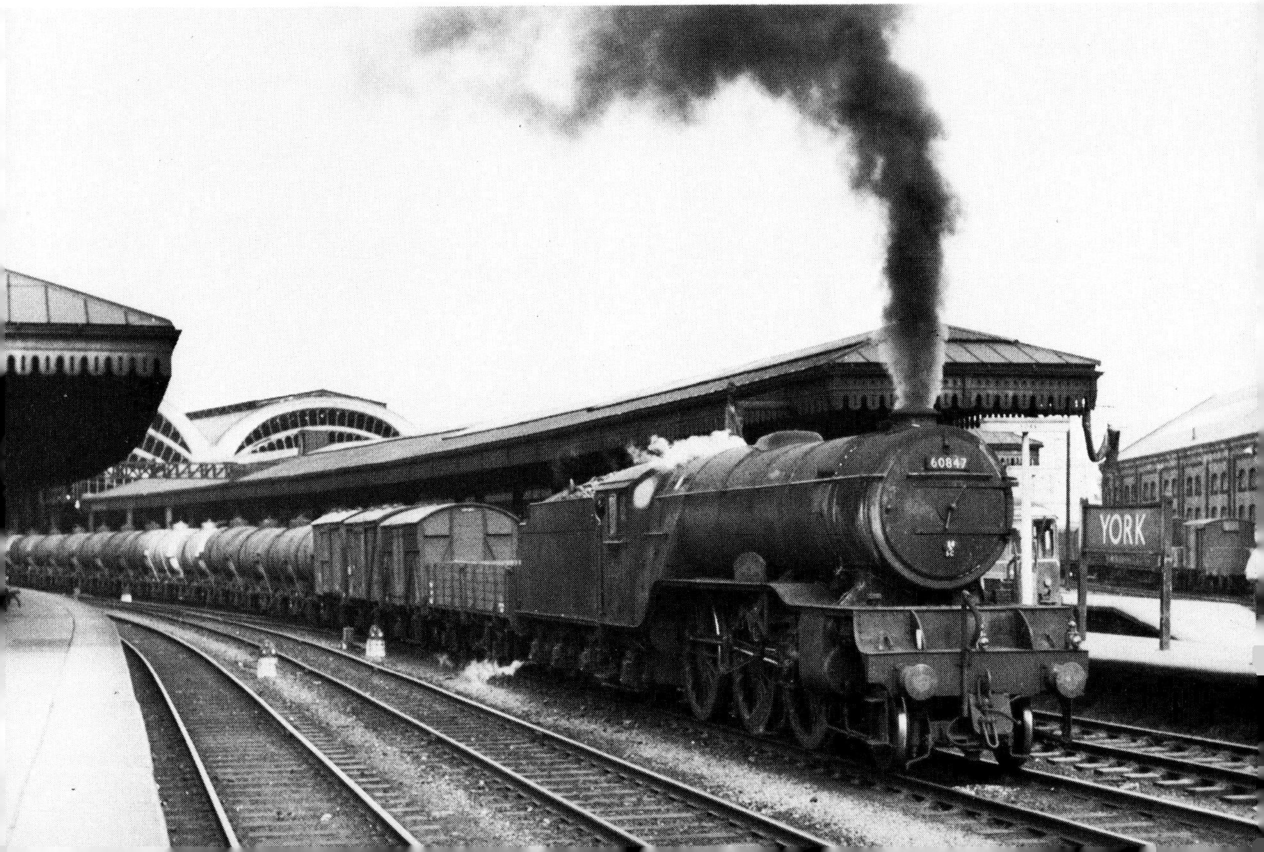
60847
YORK

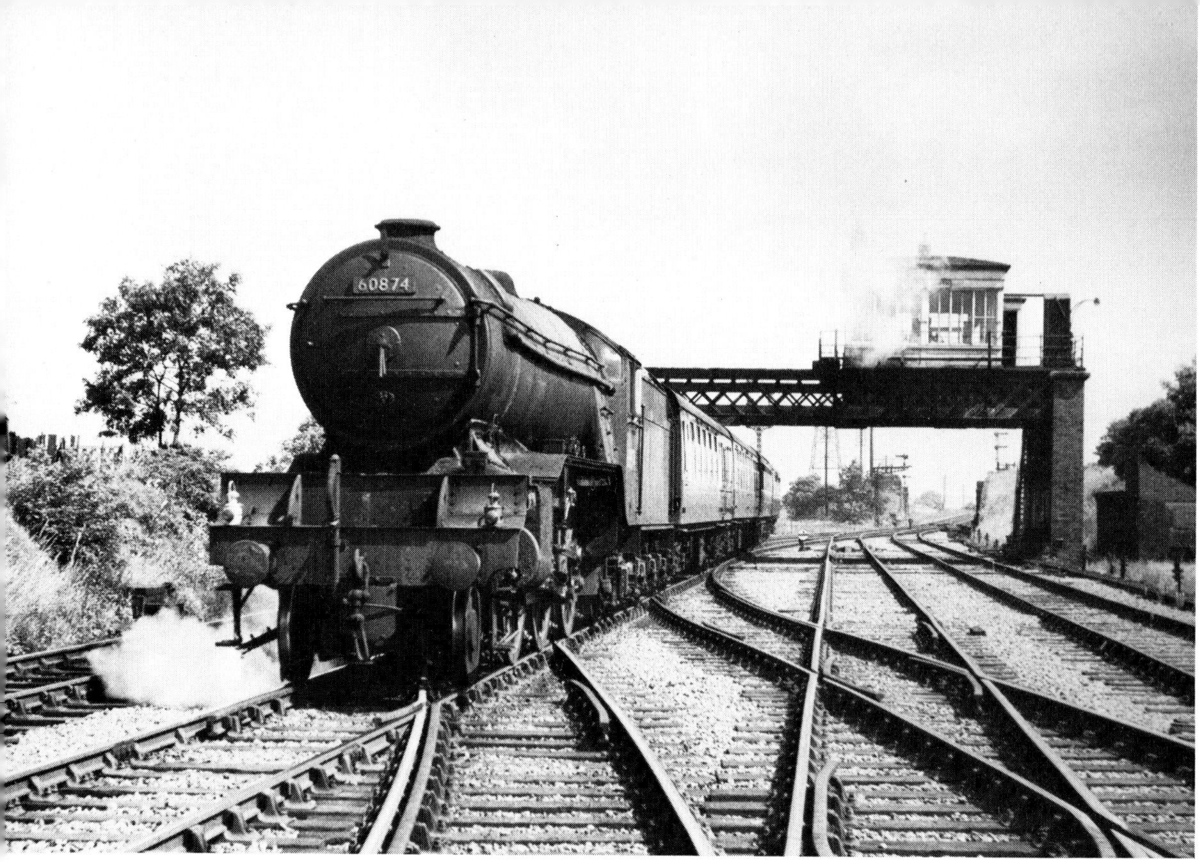
60874

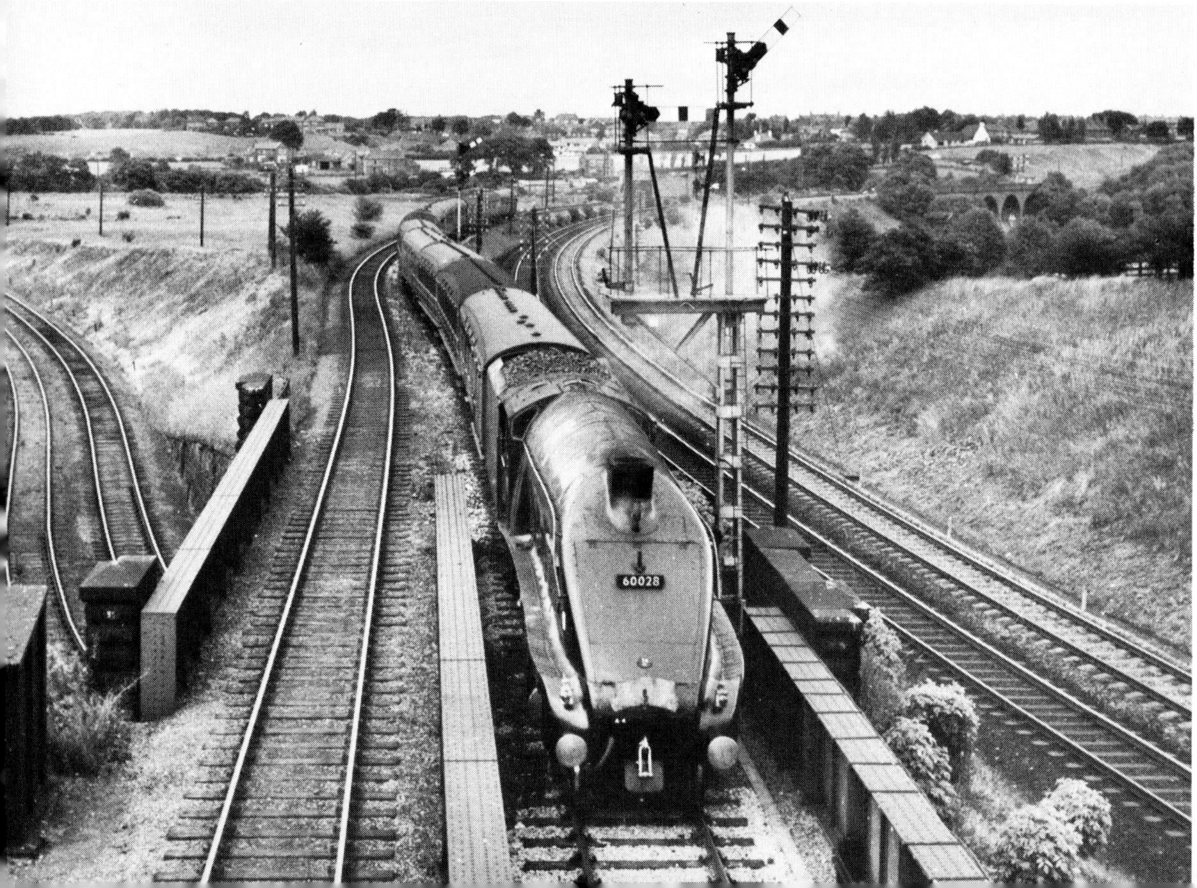
60028

Above left: Class V2 No. 60874 passing Penshaw North box on the 'old main line' on an up Sunday diversion on 12 July 1959. The train is coming off the Victoria Bridge over the Wear, with the line from Sunderland coming in on the right./*Ian S. Carr*

Left: Class A4 4-6-2 No. 60028 *Walter K. Whigham* taking the Bishop Auckland line at Relly Mill Junction, south of Durham, on a Sunday diversion. The main line south to Ferryhill is on the right, with the Baxter Wood-Bridge House connection passing below the Bishop Auckland line./*Ian S. Carr*

Top: Class A4 4-6-2 No. 60022 *Mallard* on the Victoria Bridge over the Wear on a Newcastle-Kings Cross train diverted because of Sunday engineering works on the Team Valley line, 19 July 1959./*Ian S. Carr*

Above: Class A1 4-6-2 No. 60147 *North Eastern* at Gateshead shed./*BR*

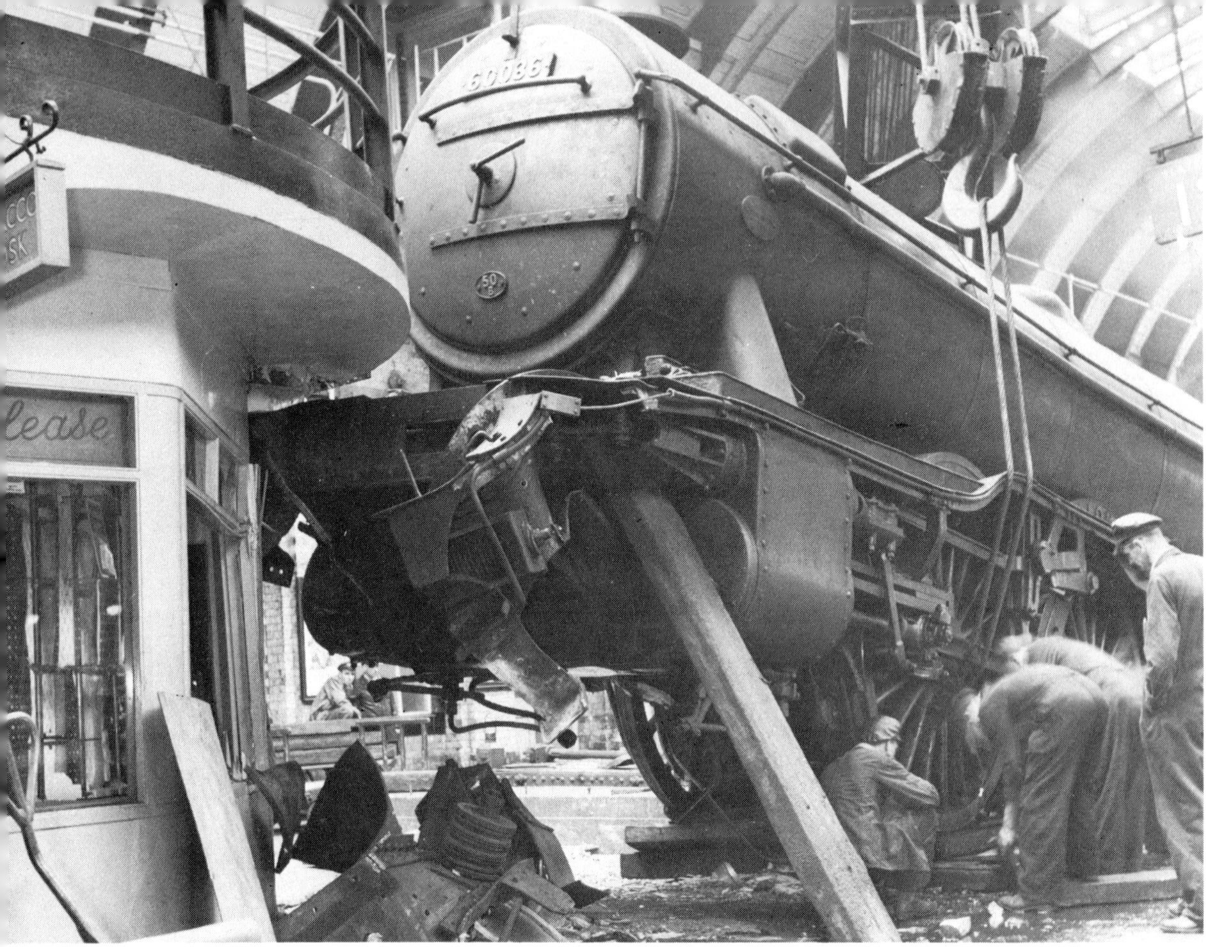
lease

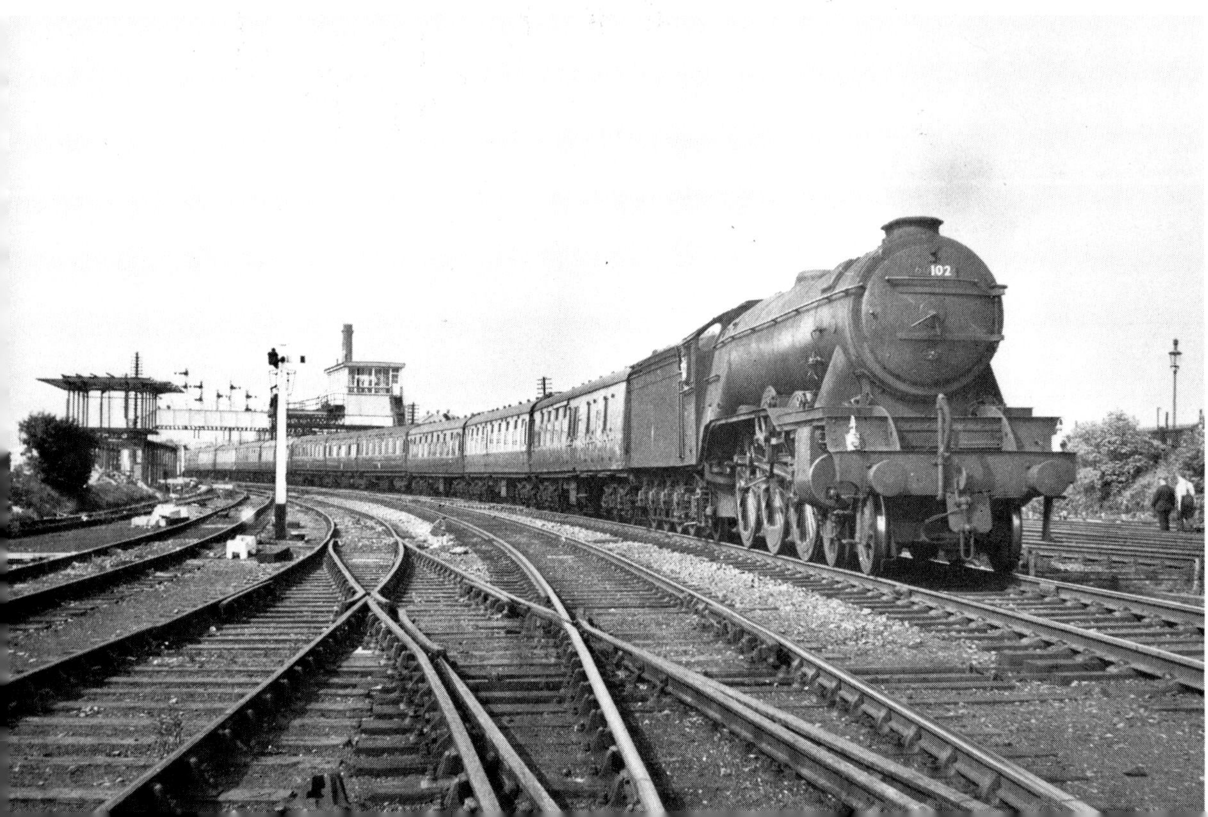
102

Left: Class A3 No. 60036 *Colombo* after the buffer-stop collision at York on 4 August 1958./*Author's Collection*

Below left: Class A3 No. 60102 *Sir Frederick Banbury* taking the Washington line at Pelaw Junction on a Sunday diversion. /*Ian S. Carr*

Below: Class V2 No. 60968 and Class 4MTT No. 42073 at Newcastle on 19 April 1955./*Author's Collection*

Bottom: The 'Flying Scotsman' stopped at York, with the fireman on the telephone to the signal box. The engine is No. 60014 *Silver Link,* the prototype A4, on 1 September 1956./*K. Hoole*

1960-1964

In spite of the introduction of diesel locomotives the year 1960 was notable for the excellent work performed by steam engines. This was because on numerous occasions a steam locomotive was called upon to replace a non-available, or non-working, diesel and went on to complete the diagram in diesel timings. For instance A4 No 60022 *Mallard* worked the down 'Flying Scotsman' from Kings Cross to Newcastle and the 5.0pm return on six consecutive days, covering 3,216 miles exclusive of running to shed etc. Thus the short turn-round time of 135min allowed for the diesel had to suffice for the A4 – an allowance unheard of in full steam days. On the other hand most of the main-line trains were still on steam timings, so that if a diesel locomotive was provided it had time well in hand – provided everything worked!

A sign that the days of steam were not yet over came with the fitting of a double chimney to V2 No 60963 in February 1960. But an ominous portent of the decreasing importance of the Gresley Pacifics was the transfer of some from their traditional duties on the East Coast main line to the former Midland Railway shed at Holbeck (Leeds) for working to Carlisle.

Royal Trains on the main line invariably produced spotlessly clean and gleaming locomotives, but three such trains in one day was distinctly unusual and a sight not to be forgotten, especially when diesel engine haulage was spurned in favour of the old reliable steam locomotive. This occurred on 8 August 1961 when the Duke of Kent married Miss Katherine Worsley in York Minster in the presence of the Queen. The event required the Royal Train and two Guest trains from Kings Cross to York, thence empty to Malton, returning from Malton to Kings Cross with a two-minute stop at York to change crews. Each train was worked by a Kings Cross A4 Pacific, No 60003 *Andrew K. McCosh* on the 8.40am Guests' train, No 60015 *Quicksilver* on the 9.15am Guests' train, and No 60028 *Walter K. Whigham* on the 10.15am Royal Train. Each locomotive was serviced at York shed and then ran light to Malton tender-first, the Royal Train engine on its own, and the two guest train engines coupled together. From York to Malton and back the engines were manned by York crews, and the three sets of Kings

Cross men did an out-and-home duty in each case, resting at York during the afternoon.

A1 No 60145 was provided as emergency engine at Selby for the down trains, and A1 No 60129 at York for both down and up trains: Type 4 diesels Nos D281 and D284 were stand-by engines at Malton, and V2 No 60879 was also available, all three after working the empty trains from York. Also standing by at Malton was Stanier 4-6-0 No 44896 on the local tool vans, ready for any minor mishap. The York breakdown train, with engine attached, was booked to be at the ready all day.

All the journeys were performed without any trouble, although at Malton there was some difficulty with a North Eastern water crane which became jammed on the side of an A4 tender when the crew decided to top up the tank!

The summer of 1962 saw notable developments in locomotive working on the East Coast main line, utilising to a greater extent the diesel locomotives which had been delivered since 1958. The English Electric 2,000hp engines had settled down on the Newcastle-Liverpool workings, although failures were still occurring far too often, and the 'Peaks' on the Newcastle-Bristol services, but it was the English Electric 3,300hp 'Deltic' locomotives which eventually lifted East Coast speed to new heights. These 22 engines were delivered between February 1961 and April 1962 and were allocated as follows:

Finsbury Park Nos D9001/3/7/9/12/5/8/20
Gateshead Nos D9002/5/8/11/4/7
Haymarket Nos D9000/4/6/10/3/6/9/21

Although the 'Deltics' had been working East Coast expresses for some time it was in the summer 1962 timetable, with its accelerated timings, that complicated new rosters were introduced.

Great publicity was made of the fact that the 'Flying Scotsman' was celebrating its centenary by timing it to Edinburgh in six hours from Kings Cross, but this was, of course, exactly the same time taken by the steam-hauled 'Coronation' 25 years earlier! (For a typical 'Deltic' roster see Appendix 2)

The Newcastle-York-Birmingham-Bristol workings were operated by three 2,500hp Sulzer locomotives from Gateshead, and four from Bath Road, Bristol, with an additional Bristol working to Newcastle on Saturdays at 10.20am, returning at 8.10am from Newcastle on a Monday morning. A Midland Lines engine worked the 12.50am Sheffield-Newcastle on a Sunday and worked through from Newcastle to Bristol on the following evening's Bristol 'mail'. (See Appendix 3)

With the introduction of through diesel locomotive workings between Newcastle and Liverpool, English Electric 2,000hp locomotives were used from each end: Edge Hill (Liverpool) units worked the 9.0am Liverpool-Newcastle and the 3.16pm return, and the 11.0am from Liverpool and the 4.47pm return, with Gateshead engines on the 8.45am and 9.42am from Newcastle, returning from Liverpool at 3.0pm and 5.5pm respectively.

With diesel traction those trains running via Harrogate were rerouted via Wetherby to avoid the locomotive having to run round its train at Leeds, which was necessary with the use of the Arthington route. The trains running via York were not affected. However, with the closure of the Cross Gates-Wetherby-Harrogate route in January 1964 the trains serving Harrogate were diverted back to the Arthington route and a reversal was necessary at Leeds, where the locomotive ran round its train. In steam days, when the Arthington route was used, the LNER engine came off the east end of the train as the LMS engine coupled on at the opposite end. Three years later came the closure of the Harrogate-Ripon-Northallerton line (the old 'Leeds Northern' route) and thus all Newcastle-Liverpool trains had to run via York. From the winter 1962/3 timetable the Newcastle-Liverpool services were taken over by the Sulzer 2,500hp locomotives – the 'Peaks'.

A York engine working through unchanged to Inverness was unheard of in steam days, but with the introduction of diesel locomotives it became a regular feature. This diagram was operated by a York English Electric 2,000hp unit on the York-Inverness car sleeper, which ran on Fridays and Sundays northbound, leaving York at 9.50pm and arriving at Inverness at 7.35am on Saturdays (ten minutes earlier on Mondays). After refuelling and inspection at Inverness the return departure was at 9.45pm (9.50pm in the public timetable) on Saturdays and Mondays, arriving at York at 7.41am on Sundays and 7.12am on Tuesdays. The service also operated on Wednesdays northbound and Thursdays southbound during the peak weeks of the summer.

Another interesting summer service was that between Glasgow, Edinburgh, Newcastle and Scarborough, which did not pass through York. More by accident than design this service ran for the last time in 1962.

Branching off to the east at Pilmoor, between Thirsk and York, was a single line branch to Gilling and Malton, part of which lost its local passenger train service in 1931. At Malton, by means of a double reversal, access could be gained to the York-Scarborough line. Scarborough has long been popular with holidaymakers from Scotland and many of them travel south to spend their summer break at this East Coast resort. To cater for this traffic, and also to serve Tyneside, there were in 1962 four Saturday trains in each direction between Glasgow, Newcastle and Scarborough, all of which ran via Gilling except for the Fridays only 11.20pm from Glasgow, which ran via York. Routeing the remaining seven trains via Gilling reduced the congestion at York and required the use of only one engine per train, instead of the two that would have been necessary in steam days if they had run via York, where reversal would have been necessary. Three or four additional trains were required on certain Saturdays to cater for the Glasgow Fair holiday period and most of these used the Gilling route.

To work the regular trains (in 1962) York provided two B1 4-6-0s and one V2 2-6-2; Blaydon turned out one B1; and Gateshead two V2s. The two Gateshead engines worked trains from Newcastle to Sheffield (Midland) on the Fridays, then back to York, running out light to Scarborough on the Saturday morning, ready to travel as far as Newcastle.

By the summer of 1962 it was not always possible to provide an engine of the type rostered for the duty and occasionally Pacifics of various types appeared, with increasing use of EE 2,000hp diesel-electric locomotives. However, perhaps the strangest engine to work over the single-line Gilling Branch was a 9F 2-10-0, which replaced a failed engine.

On the night of 19 March 1963 the 8.0pm Sunderland-York parcels train conveying hundreds of parcels from a mail order warehouse was derailed at Pilmoor, and as twelve of the thirteen bogie vans distributed themselves over the four tracks they destroyed the Gilling branch junction. Parcels were scattered everywhere as some of the vans broke up and the parcels were collected by railway staff and sent on to York by road. To get traffic on the main line moving again as quickly as possible the junction was relaid with plain track, but when the time came to resume this long-established route to Scarborough it was decided not to restore the junction but to reroute the trains via York. With the greater use of diesel locomotives this became a simple task as it was possible to run the engine round its train at York and use the same machine to work the train forward.

The last of the trains to use the Gilling route was the 10.50am from Scarborough to Newcastle on 8

September 1962, headed by B16/2 4-6-0 No 61421. Because this was getting near the end of the summer season there was no corresponding up train on that day.

Two further interesting summer Saturday workings were the Saltburn-Glasgow and Whitley Bay-Glasgow trains. The former was worked from Saltburn to Edinburgh by a Stockton B1, with Stockton men as far as Newcastle and Gateshead men forward. In the return direction it was covered by Gateshead men with a Haymarket Pacific as far as Newcastle, and by Stockton men with a V2 to Saltburn. The workings were taken over by Thornaby when Stockton shed closed. The Whitley Bay train was worked to Morpeth by a Heaton V3 2-6-2T; at Morpeth a Heaton V2 was attached to the rear and hauled the train to Edinburgh.

The non-stop 'Elizabethan' last ran on 9 September 1961, when the up train was worked by Haymarket A4 No 60009 *Union of South Africa*, and the down train by the most famous A4 No 60022 *Mallard*, of Kings Cross. In the 1962 (summer) public timetable the 'Elizabethan' was shown as running non-stop once again but with the use of 'Deltic' locomotives it did, in fact, stop at Newcastle in both directions to change crews: from 11.40am to 11.42am in the up direction, and from 1.31½pm to 1.33½pm in the down. Thus after 34 years (except for 1940 to 1947 inclusive) this world-beating run came to an end. For the whole of the post-war period during which the non-stop ran it had been the sole responsibility of the Haymarket and Kings Cross Gresley A4 Pacifics, some of which worked the train day after day, up one day and down the next, with amazing regularity.

Although Gateshead crews were involved in the working of the non-stop from 1928 to 1939 they were not used for the post-war operations, when all the duties were covered by Kings Cross and Haymarket crews, and this persisted after the introduction of the Newcastle stop in 1962. The Haymarket men worked the up 'Elizabethan' to Newcastle, and took over the down train for their return working, whilst the Kings Cross men working the down train returned home on the next day's 1.22am up. The men for the up 'Elizabethan' worked down from Kings Cross on the 4.0pm 'Talisman' the previous day.

In 1963 the 'Elizabethan' service was abandoned and the 'Flying Scotsman' once again became the premier mid-morning train between London and Edinburgh, with a time of six hours in both directions (Saturdays excepted), stopping only at Newcastle. The same timing applied to the afternoon up and down 'Talisman' (4.0pm from Edinburgh and 4.0pm from Kings Cross), but the morning down train now required 6hr 19min because of stops at Grantham, Darlington, Newcastle and Berwick, and the up 6hr 15min with stops at Berwick, Newcastle and Darlington.

The 'Yorkshire Pullman' received new cars on 9 January 1961; the 'Tyne-Tees Pullman' on 16 January 1961, and the 'Queen of Scots' on 10 April 1961. The 1st class Parlour Cars carried jewel names, and the 1st class Kitchen Cars bird names: however, the 30 year-old brake 2nds were retained. After only three years with the new stock it was decided to withdraw the 'Queen of Scots' and from 15 June 1964 to replace it with a new 'White Rose Pullman' running between Kings Cross and Leeds Central in roughly the same timings, although there was some acceleration. The official announcement regarding the ending of this well-known train said that 'with the continued improvement of passenger train services between England and Scotland by the East Coast route the number of travellers over the Leeds-Glasgow section of the 'Queen of Scots' run has declined during recent years until the continuance of this northern section of the service can no longer be justified'. This was, in fact, another nail in the coffin being prepared for the old Leeds Northern route between Harrogate and Northallerton, which closed three years later. The set of Pullman cars released by the withdrawal of the 'Queen of Scots' was used as the 1st class accommodation on the 8.0am down 'Talisman' and the 4.0pm return from Edinburgh.

New coaching stock (known as Project XP 64) was introduced on the 8.0am up 'Talisman' and the 4.0pm return working from Kings Cross on 15 June 1964. In addition to new interior arrangements the exterior was finished with pale blue lower panels, setting the trend for the Inter-City livery subsequently standardised by British Rail.

The early 1960s saw the slaughter of the East Coast Pacifics – the locomotives which had been the mainstay of the line for 40 years. As many as 55 Pacifics were withdrawn in 1963 and the last went to the scrap-heap in 1966. This was the pace of Class A1, A1/1, A2, A2/1, A2/2, A2/3, and A4 withdrawals:

Year	Withdrawn	Total at 31 Dec.
1958	–	202
1959	3	199
1960	4	195
1961	10	185
1962	40	145
1963	55	90

Year	withdrawn	total at 31 Dec
1964	41	49
1965	37	12
1966	12	Nil

Other classes which became extinct in the period 1960 to 1964 were: 1960, B16/1; 1962, J21, J26, J39, K3 and Q7; 1964, B16/2 and B16/3. The B1 4-6-0s also suffered severely and from one withdrawal in 1961 the number had jumped to 120 withdrawn in 1962! These were not only North Eastern Region engines but were distributed over most of the former LNER lines. Another well-known class which disappeared rapidly was the V2 2-6-2, so commonly known as 'Green Arrows' after the original engine of the class turned out from Doncaster in 1936. They were all withdrawn in the space of five years, thus:

Year	Withdrawn	Total at 31 Dec.
1961	–	184
1962	69	115
1963	43	72
1964	32	40
1965	26	14
1966	14	Nil

The rapid introduction of diesel locomotives, and the consequent reduction in the number of steam locomotives, led to the transfer from Heaton in June 1963 of its allocation of steam engines. However, it remained in use as a sub-shed to Gateshead, carrying out repairs and housing engines which Gateshead's cramped accommodation was unable to handle. On the day that Heaton closed as a main shed the empty coaching stock workings between Heaton Carriage Sidings and Newcastle Central were handed over to Type 2 diesel haulage, but this lasted for less than three days and the familiar V3 2-6-2T had to be recalled to resume their old jobs. This continued until August 1964 when Heaton closed to steam locomotives. Except for a few minor exceptions steam traction of passenger trains in the Newcastle area ceased with the introduction of the winter timetable on 7 September 1964. Haymarket shed ceased handling steam locomotives at the same time. However, Pacifics and V2s were still required to replace diesel locomotives. Gateshead's last A4, No 60001 *Sir Ronald Matthews*, was withdrawn on 6 October 1964.

In its final year, 1947, the LNER painted J71 No 8286 and J72 No 8680 green for pilot duties at York and Newcastle respectively, and this livery lasted until 1952. In 1960 the idea was revived and two J72 were chosen to be repainted in North Eastern green – No 68723 for Newcastle and No 68736 for York. When displaced from York in the following year No 68736 moved to Newcastle to join No 68723 and the pair remained on pilot duties at Newcastle until they were displaced by diesel shunters in September 1963. Their clean condition, colourful green livery and polished brass made a brave sight in a world of dirty steam locomotives and unreliable diesels.

Improvements to the signalling system were taking place along the main line and major colour-light installations were introduced at Tollerton and Tweedmouth in 1961, and at Gateshead in 1962. One signalling item not connected with modernisation which caught the headlines in June 1963 was the collapse of a gantry spanning all the tracks at Ferryhill. Main line traffic was stopped completely and had to be diverted until the large gantry could be cleared.

In May 1964 a micro-waye radio telephone link was established to link railway installations at York, Darlington and Newcastle. A 'dish' aerial was constructed on the roof of the HQ Offices building at York and from there radio signals were beamed to a repeater station near Thirsk, which passed on the signals to Darlington; from here the signals were transmitted to a tower-mounted 'dish' aerial at Tyne Yard via a repeater station near Ferryhill. Initially 159 speech channels were provided, with facilities to extend to 300 when warranted.

Above: Class A4 No. 60032 *Gannet* entering Waverley station Edinburgh, on the down 'Elizabethan' 124 min. late due to a hot box on 1 September 1956./*Ian S. Carr*

Below: A B16/3 (Thompson rebuild) 4-6-0 approaching Durham on a down goods on 3 March 1962./*Ian S. Carr*

*Above:*Class A3 4-6-2 No. 60065 *Knight of Thistle* on an up goods and Type 4 diesel No. D172 on a Liverpool-Newcastle train cross Durham Viaduct on 23 July 1963./*Ian S. Carr*

Below: Class A4 No. 60032 *Gannet* passing York on the down 'Elizabethan' on 26 August 1960./*Ian S. Carr*

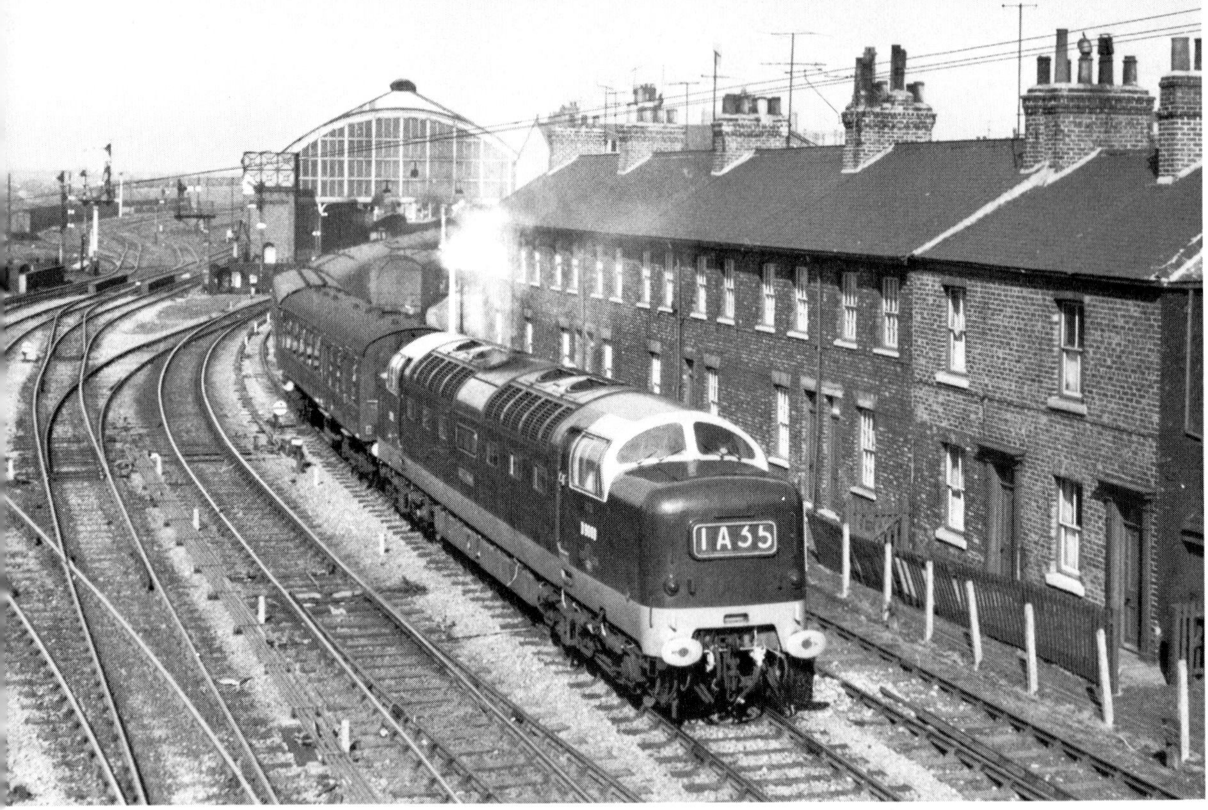
IA35

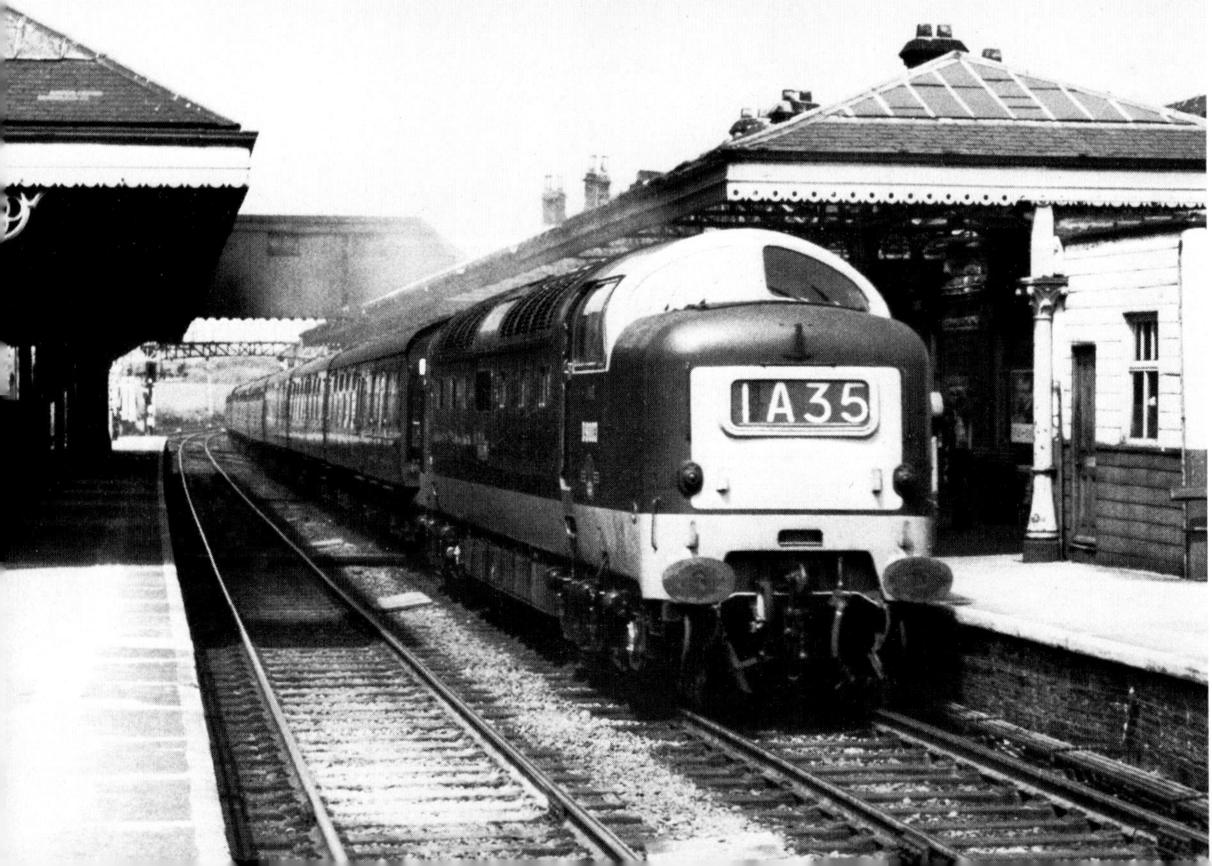
IA35

Above left: 'Deltic' No. D9009 *Alycidon* leaving Stockton on a diverted Edinburgh-Kings Cross train on 1 April 1962./*Ian S. Carr*

Left: 'Deltic' No. D9003 *Meld* passing Alnmouth on an up express on 2 June 1963./*Ian S. Carr*

Top: Class A4 No. 60028 *Walter K. Whigham* on the Royal Train for the wedding of the Duke of Kent at York on 8 June 1961. /*Author's Collection*

Above: Type 2 diesel Nos. D5103 and D5107 and Class B1 No 61103 leaving York on the Red Bank stock train on 27 August 1961./*N. E. W. Skinner*

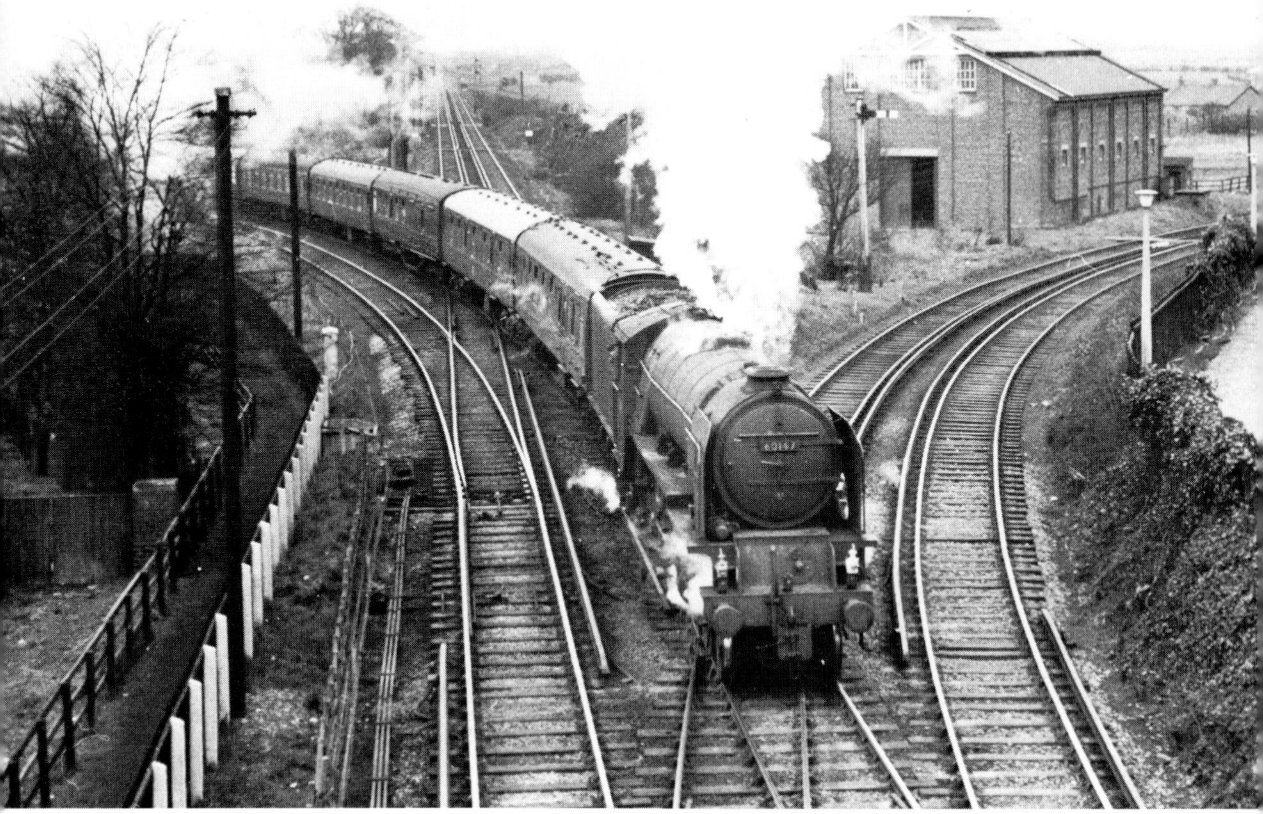

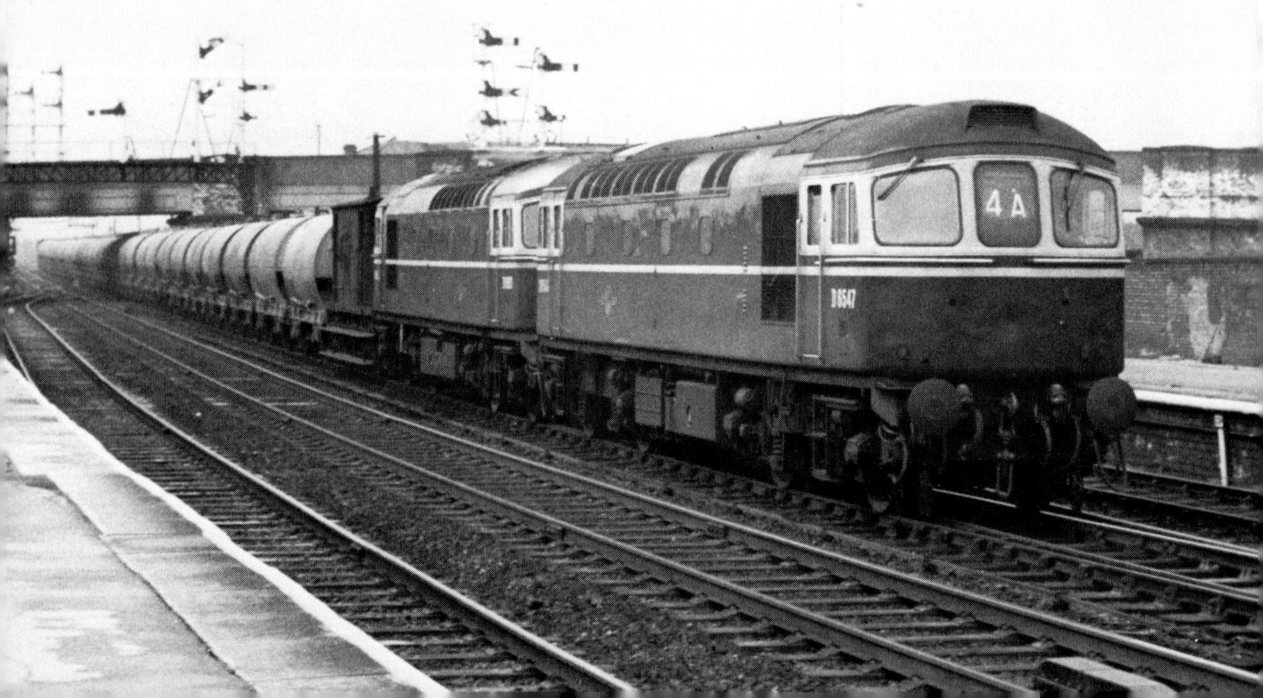
4A
D6547

Above left: Class A1 4-6-2 No. 60147 *North Eastern* coming off the north-west curve at Benton to join the old Blyth & Tyne route into Newcastle via South Gosforth on a Sunday diversion on 15 April 1962./*Ian S. Carr*

Left: Southern Region diesels Nos. D6547 and D6563 passing Selby with a bulk cement train on 13 June 1962./*Ian S. Carr*

Top: Class B16/3 No. 61472 approaching Durham on the 8.40am Scarborough-Glasgow train on 23 July 1960./*Ian S. Carr*

Above: The Victoria Bridge over the Wear, built by the Durham Junction Railway to form part of the 'old main line'. 28 August 1964./*Ian S. Carr*

Left: Class V3 2-6-2T No. 67687 piloting Class A3 4-6-2 No. 60050 *Persimmon* climbing Seaton Bank with a Newcastle-Kings Cross train diverted via Wellfield on 28 May 1961. */Ian S. Carr*

Below: Class J27 0-6-0 No. 65812 near Durham on 19 August 1960./*Ian S. Carr*

Right: Class Q7 0-8-0 No. 63461 on an up goods between Durham and Relly Mill./*Ian S. Carr*

Below right: Class B1 4-6-0 No. 61176 near Durham on the 08.05 Glasgow-Scarborough train on 29 July 1961./*Ian S. Carr*

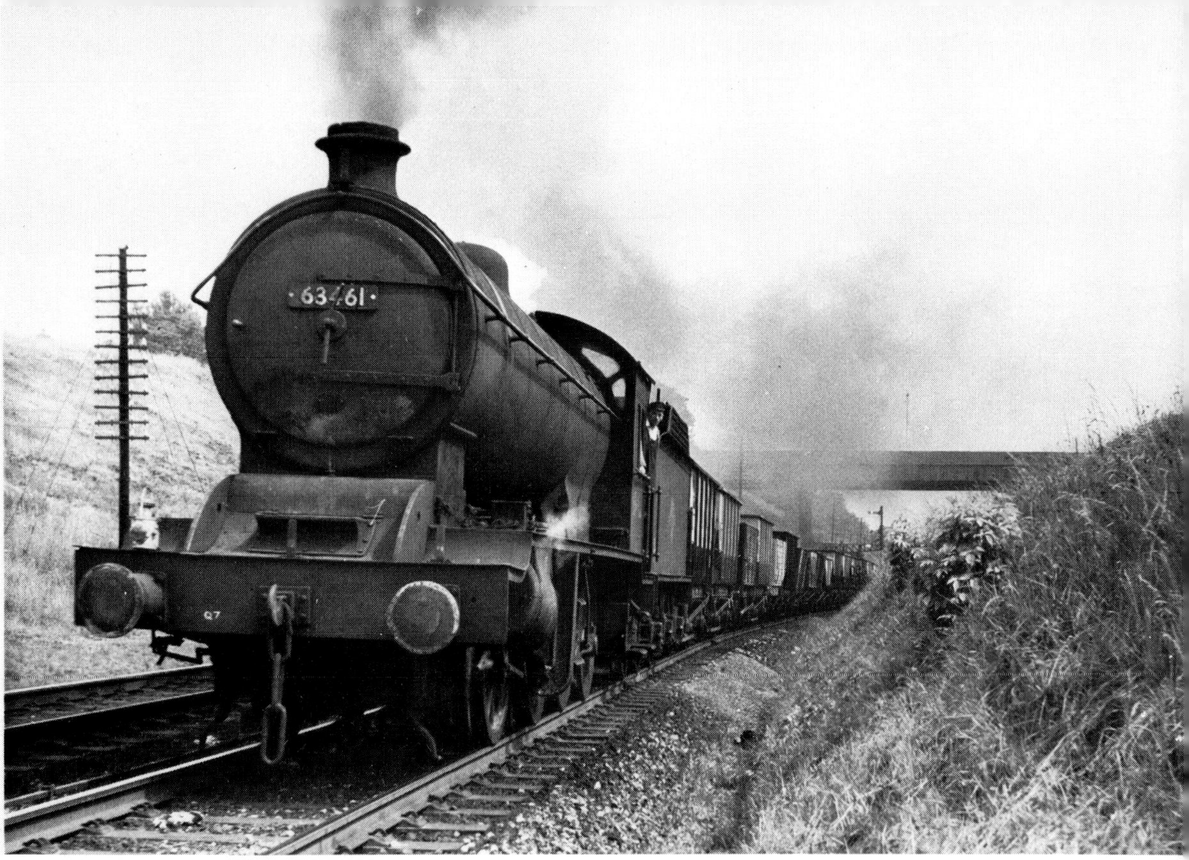

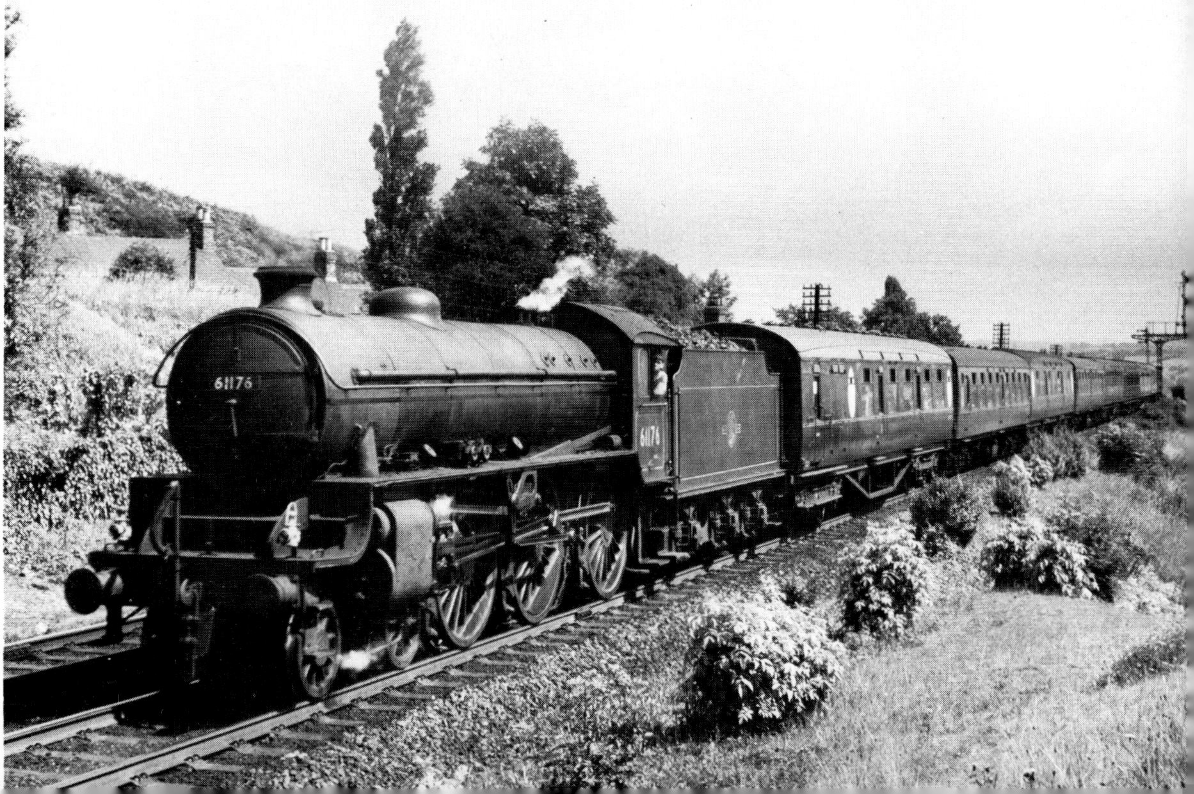
61176

Above: Class Q6 0-8-0 No. 63407 takes the Team Valley line at Newton Hall Junction, north of Durham on 21 August 1961. */Ian S. Carr*

Below: Class A2/3 4-6-2 No. 60511 *Airborne* leaving Newcastle Central on a Birmingham train on 9 April 1960./*Ian S. Carr*

Right: Class A3 No. 60065 *Knight of Thistle* leaving Newcastle with the up 'Heart of Midlothian' on 13 April 1960./*Ian S. Carr*

Above: Class A4 4-6-2 No. 60027 *Merlin* passes Heaton with the up 'Elizabethan' on 1 September 1960./*Ian S. Carr*

Below: 'Deltic' No. D9019 coming off the Royal Border Bridge and into Berwick station on a Glasgow train on 30 August 1962./ *Ian S. Carr*

1965-1969

1965 was officially the last year of steam traction on the East Coast main line and on 31 December the North Eastern Region ran a steam-hauled relief train from York to Newcastle and back to signify the formal last steam train. This was hauled by Class A1 No 60145.

Gateshead shed was closed to steam on 20 March 1965, and in the same year work commenced on rebuilding Haymarket shed. However, steam locomotives were still being called upon to replace failed diesel locomotives, and on the north-east coast steam engines were still slogging away (albeit in a very run-down condition) on coal trains.

1966 saw further changes and the remaining twelve LNER Pacifics were eliminated, including A1 Nos 60124 and 60145, both of Darlington, where they were the emergency engines. By this time these were the only two Pacifics working on the North Eastern section of the main line, the others (A2 Nos 60528/30/2, A3 No 60052, and A4 Nos 60004/7/9/19/23/34) being stationed in Scotland, all at Aberdeen or Dundee except for No 60052 at St. Margarets.

It was planned to close Darlington shed (excluding the diesel depot) on 31 December 1965, but this was not possible and it actually closed on 27 March 1966: on the same day the two A1 Pacifics were withdrawn but on 17 April No 60145 was re-instated and allocated to York, only to be withdrawn for good on 19 June.

The town of Darlington suffered a second blow when, only a week after the shed had been shut down, the Works at North Road also closed. These Works, which developed into the main centre for NER, LNER, and North Eastern Region locomotive repairs, had been established in the final days of the Stockton & Darlington Railway and were opened on 1 January 1863, only a few months before the Stockton & Darlington was taken over by the North Eastern. Many famous types of locomotives had been built at Darlington, especially in the twentieth century, including R1 4-4-0 (introduced 1908); S2 4-6-0 (1911); S3 4-6-0 (1919); T2 0-8-0 (1913); V/09 4-4-2 (1910); Z1 4-4-2 (1914); Raven 4-6-2 (1922); D49 (1927); K3 (1924); and J39 (1926), etc.

In the summer of 1965 the timing of the 'Flying Scotsman' was reduced by a further five minutes to 5hr 55min in each direction, including a stop at Newcastle. From 18 April 1966 it was reduced yet again, to 5hr 50min, giving an average speed of 67.3mph.

On 1 January 1967 the North Eastern Region became part of the Eastern Region and the title 'North Eastern' was dropped after 113 years' use – first as North Eastern Railway, then the North Eastern Area of the LNER, and finally the North Eastern Region of BR. However, the former NER offices at York became the headquarters of the new Region, together with a new office block – Hudson House, built in the yard of the original station at York, which was replaced by the present station in 1877.

On 6 March 1967, with the introduction of the new timetable, the 'Deltic' diagrams were revised. By this time the down morning 'Talisman' had been debased by the introduction of stops at Hitchin, Peterborough, Grantham, Doncaster and York, defeating one of the original objects, which was to provide a fast business service to Tyneside. Consequently a new fast train was put on leaving Kings Cross at 07.55, five minutes before the 'Talisman', and stopping only at Darlington. Arrival time at Newcastle was 11.45, 3hr 50min from Kings Cross, beating the pre-war 'Silver Jubilee' timing by 10 min. A similar working in the up direction left Newcastle at 16.45 and arrived at Kings Cross at 20.35. The 230 miles between London and Darlington were covered in 189min down and 190min up.

With this timetable the 'White Rose Pullman' was withdrawn and the Hull portion of the 'Yorkshire Pullman' commenced to run as a separate train under the mundane title of the 'Hull Pullman'. The up train was accelerated by 21min to 3hr 9min, and the down by 13min to 3hr 28min for the 196miles, due partly to the saving in time at Doncaster, where the Hull vehicles previously had to be attached or detached from the Harrogate and Bradford portions.

Steam in the north-east was finally vanquished in 1967 after 142years of service to the North Eastern, its predecessors and its successors, the fateful day being 9 September 1967. On that day the following locomotives were withdrawn:

North Blyth 4MT 2-6-0(5)
Tyne Dock K1 2-6-0(4)
West Hartlepool Q6 0-8-0(2), WD 2-8-0(7)
Sunderland J27 0-6-0(5) Q6 0-8-0(1) WD 2-8-0(5)

In addition K1 No 62005 was transferred from Tyne Dock to Holbeck. The three Q6 engines and the five J27s were the last 0-8-0s and the last 0-6-0s respectively to remain in BR service, and four of the J27s and the three Q6s were the last North Eastern-built locomotives, and the last standard-gauge pre-grouping locomotives, in service. J27 No 65894 was purchased for preservation and No 63395, after being sold for scrap, was also bought for preservation, both by the North Eastern Locomotive Preservation Group. Both are now running on the North Yorkshire Moors Railway.

This left a pocket of steam locomotives in the West Riding, at Holbeck, Low Moor, Normanton, and Royston. It was eliminated early in November except for K1 No 62005 at Holbeck, which was not condemned until 30 December 1967. This engine is also at work on the North Yorkshire Moors line between Grosmont and Pickering.

The following table illustrates the decline of steam on BR during the period 1959 to 1968:

31 December	Steam Locos	Diesel Locos
1959	14,457	1,799
1960	13,276	2,550
1961	11,691	3,179
1962	8,767	3,683
1963	7,050	4,060
1964	4,973	4,462
1965	2,987	4,811
1966	1,689	4,961
1967	362	4,742
1968	3*	4,325

*Narrow gauge

On 15 July 1967 the up 'North Briton' was derailed by a broken rail whilst running at about 75mph between Acklington and Chevington. All the coaches were derailed but they remained in line until the speed had dropped, when the centre of the train went off the formation and into a field on the up side. Fortunately only nine passengers suffered minor injuries. The locomotive and first coach came to rest 572yds ahead of the broken rail, with a distance of 183yds separating first and second coaches.

Sixteen days later, on 31 July, a down cement train was derailed whilst travelling on the slow line south of Thirsk. The derailment commenced with the twelfth wagon and the following eight wagons ran out of the way and into a field on the down side. Unfortunately the 23rd wagon came to rest foul of the down main line on which the 12 noon Kings Cross-Edinburgh express was approaching at a speed of about 80mph. Through the cement dust thrown up by the derailment the driver of the express saw that something was amiss with the freight train and although he braked fully he was unable to stop in time. The locomotive, No DP2,

struck the derailed wagon at about 50mph, derailing the locomotive and the leading seven coaches. The first three coaches were severely damaged and torn open; seven passengers were killed and 45 injured, Fortunately the second and third coaches had their corridors on the damaged side, but the leading vehicle, a composite brake, had its compartments on the vulnerable side.

The engine, No DP2, was severely damaged. It was a 2,700hp diesel-electric owned by the English Electric Co. and on extended trial on the East Coast main line. It was manned by a Gateshead crew. The engine on the cement train was No D283, single-manned by a York driver. On this occasion the Leeds Northern line from Harrogate to Northallerton was re-opened for three days for traffic in the down direction.

Failures to couple up brake pipes have led to accidents in the north-east (Newcastle Central 1897 and Filey Holiday Camp 1956 are two that come to mind) but in the derailment which occurred at Darlington on 11 December 1968 the pipes were coupled, but coupled incorrectly. In addition the crew omitted to carry out a brake test before the train left Newcastle and consequently it was not until the brakes were required to stop the train in the platform at Darlington was it realised that the only brake power available was that on the locomotive.

The accident revealed that the coupling heads of the two pipes, supposedly incompatible, allowed the fireman to couple up (incorrectly) the brake pipe on the engine to the main reservoir pipe on the leading coach, and the main reservoir pipe on the engine to the brake pipe on the coach, this being air-braked stock with two-pipe control. The corresponding heads of the brake pipes should have been painted red, and the heads of the main reservoir pipes yellow, but although the heads of the pipes on the coach were correctly coloured the heads on the locomotive were both white, thus nullifying the safeguard provided for staff engaged on coupling up.

The train ran through Darlington Bank Top station at approximately 35mph and the engine ('Deltic' No 9017) and the first three coaches were derailed at a sand drag south of No 1 platform. This sand drag guarded the point where it was possible for an up train through the station to come into head-on collision with a down express passing outside the station – as happened at this very spot 40 years earlier.

In the early hours of 25 March 1877 the previous night's 10.30pm Edinburgh to Kings Cross was derailed on the sharp curve at Morpeth and five passengers were killed. This was due to excessive speed round the curve and 92 years later a similar derailment occured at the same site, but this time to a down train. The date was 7 May 1969, and the train was the 19.40 Kings Cross-Aberdeen – the 'Aberdonian' – which had left Kings Cross the previous evening.

As the train was approaching Morpeth the driver allowed his mind to be distracted, due to the fact that when he booked on for duty he was handed a note asking why he had dropped four minutes when working an up train some weeks previously. Because of this he failed to reduce speed to the 40mph restriction on the curve and instead the train was travelling at 80mph. All eleven coaches of the train were derailed but the locomotive rode the curve well in spite of the excessive speed, and it came to a stand 508 yds ahead of the initial derailment, still attached to the underframe of the leading vehicle – even though the body of this van had been destroyed and both bogies torn off! Five passengers and a travelling ticket collector were killed and 121 passengers were injured. In the 1877 derailment the engine was badly damaged and a rail actually went right through the smokebox as the locomotive slid along on its side. In the 1969 derailment the engine ('Deltic' No 9011) did not suffer a scratch!

It is odd that over the years nothing has been done to eliminate one of the most common accidents on British railways. This refers to the misreading of signals by a driver running on a slow line or loop, thinking he is on the fast line, taking the fast line signals and ignoring those applying to him. Thus when the loop comes to an end the engine and train is derailed at the trap points guarding the entry to the main line. There is nothing but the driver's knowledge of the line to tell him which track he is on. Such accidents which occur both during the day and during darkness have cost a number of lives and a considerable amount of money in rescuing and repairing engines and rolling stock damaged.

Two that come to mind on the main line concern C7 Atlantic No 2197 at Newton Hall on 13 June 1937 (on an excursion returning from Scar-

borough to Newcastle), and one which falls into the period under discussion. This occurred at Preston-le-Skerne, some seven miles north of Darlington, on 7 May 1965, the engine being No D350 on the 1.05am York to Newcastle (New Bridge Street) goods. This had been put in the loop to allow the 00.12 Manchester (Exchange) to Newcastle newspaper train to pass, but although the engine of the goods train went down the bank and into the field its train piled up and the wreckage was hit by the newspaper train.

When No D350 ran into the field it landed on its side on very marshy ground near the River Skerne, and great difficulty was encountered in getting it to track level again. In fact it had first to be hauled upright, then the body was removed from the bogies and lifted to track level by two cranes, followed by the bogies. The locomotive was then re-assembled and towed to Darlington. Because of the work involved the engine was not recovered until 16 days after the accident as the major operations could only be carried out at week-ends when full possession of the line could be obtained. A simple treadle-operated gong (as used in some tunnels) to remind the driver that he was on the slow line would have saved many thousands of pounds and some lives over the years!

On 1 May 1968 Alan Pegler's locomotive *Flying Scotsman* worked a special train non-stop from London to Edinburgh to commemorate the introduction of the non-stop 'Flying Scotsman' train exactly 40 years earlier. The story has often been told of how the 1968 run was narrowly accomplished: a broken rail north of Doncaster, signals at Manors (Newcastle) and a diversion on to the goods lines at Berwick almost brought the train to a halt, but persistence on the part of the Kings Cross and Gateshead crews, and the Locomotive Inspectors, finally brought success and a triumphal entry into Waverley station at Edinburgh, reached in 465min. On the return journey three days later, with only one anxious moment – signals at Tollerton – the trip was accomplished in 455min – 40 minutes less than by the non-stop 'Scotsman' of 40 years earlier.

Above: The prototype EE diesel No. DP2 derailed after a collision with derailed bulk cement wagons south of Thirsk on 31 July 1967./*J. M. Boyes*

Below: The 4,000 hp diesel prototype *Kestrel*, on trial on the East Coast main line, entering Newcastle Central west end in October 1969./*Ian S. Carr*

Above right: Speed restriction signs awaiting erection in the Durham area after track alterations on 13 December 1969. /*Ian S. Carr*

Right: 'Deltic' No. D9003 *Meld* crossing Chester-le-Street viaduct on 8 June 1969./*Ian S. Carr*

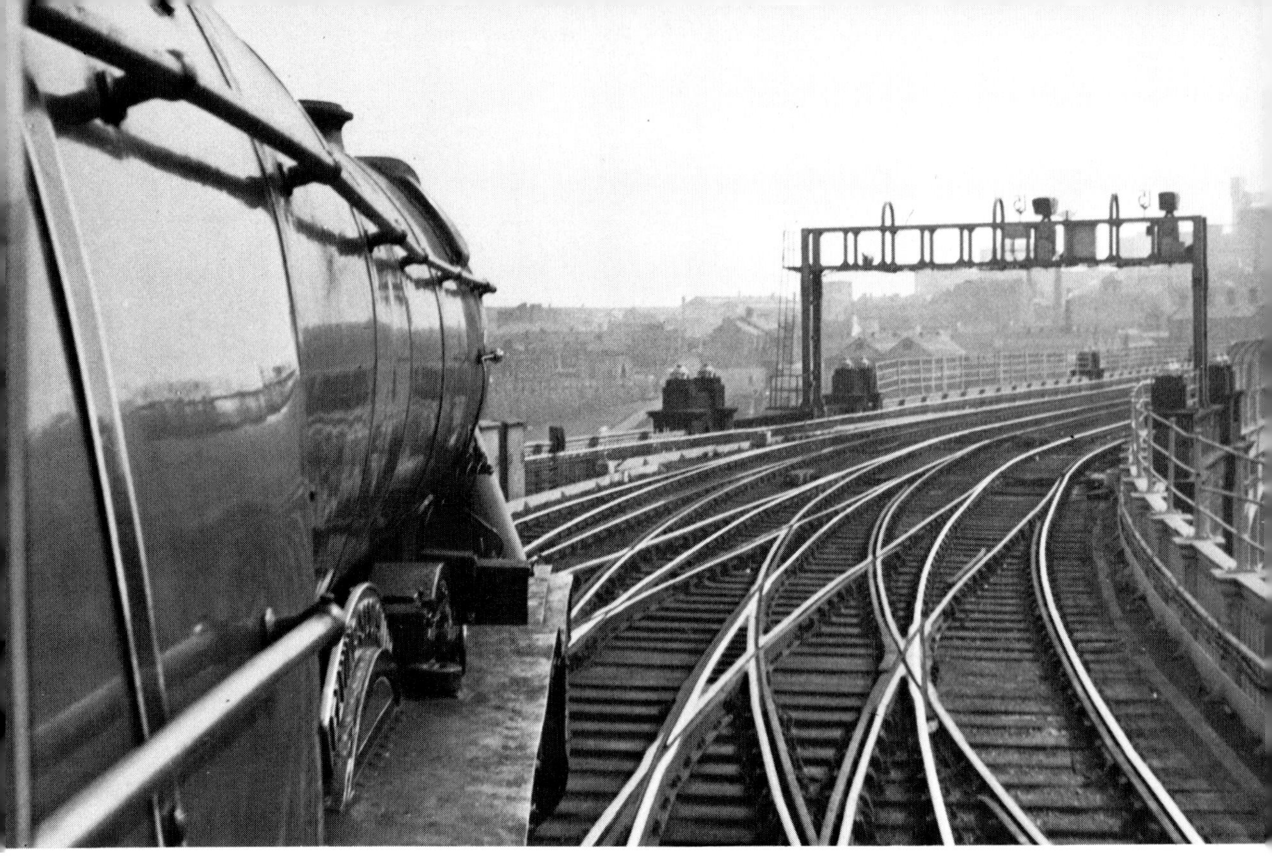

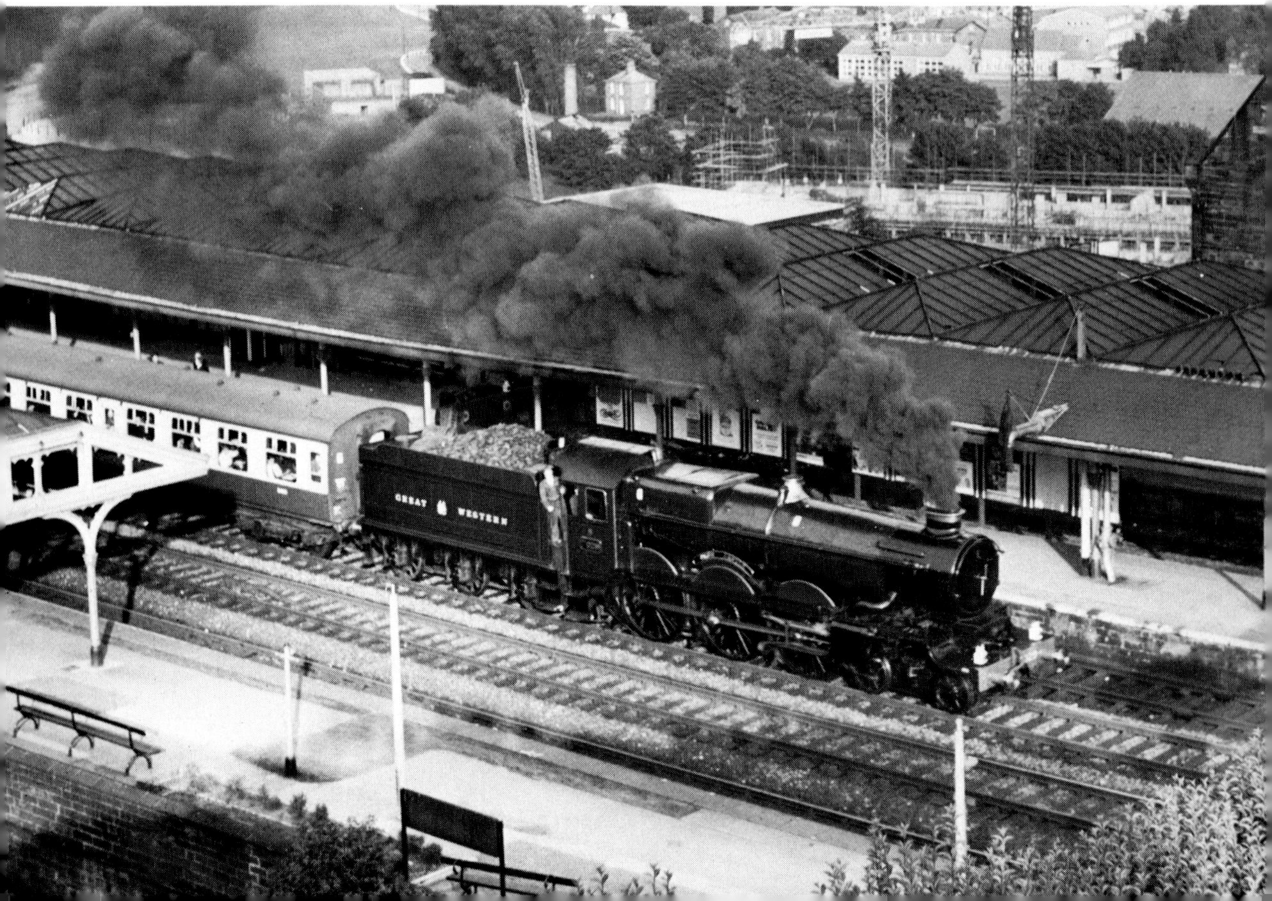
GREAT WESTERN

Above left: View from the footplate of No. 4472 *Flying Scotsman* approaching the High Level Bridge at Newcastle on 7 September 1968./*Ian S. Carr*

Left: WR 4-6-0 No. 7029 *Clun Castle* passing Durham on 10 September 1967./*Ian S. Carr*

Above: 'Deltic' No. D9008 *The Green Howards* at Gateshead MPD on 8 October 1964./*BR*

Below: Prototype diesel *Kestrel* at Newcastle Central on 29 October 1969./*Ian S. Carr*

1970-1975

On 1 January 1970 the allocation of locomotives to Eastern Region and Scottish Region sheds was as follows (see table below).

It must not be assumed that 388 diesel locomotives were required to replace 464 steam engines: for instance, Gateshead is now the only depot in the Newcastle area, providing the locomotives to cover the duties performed by seventeen other sheds on Tyneside and Wearside. Between them these sheds had an allocation of 578 engines and it was this number which the Gateshead locomotives had replaced. Needless to say, in the intervening 20 years numerous branches, sidings, and services have disappeared, considerably reducing the number of engines required anyway.

Work was still progressing on improving the main line and certain curves were being eased to allow for faster running. Between Relly Mill and Bridge House the main line was realigned; following this came the completely new curve at Newton Hall, north of Durham. Until May 1964 Newton Hall was the point where Durham-Sunderland trains diverged from the main line. Although the Sunderland line was treated as the branch it was, in fact, in being some 11 years before the Team Valley line – now the main line – came into use. From 1857 to 1868 Durham was only a wayside station on the Bishop Auckland branch, but from 1868 the section between Newton Hall Junction and Relly Mill Junction became part of the main line and as Durham happened to be between these two points it became a main-line station.

The junction at Newton Hall was taken out in November 1964 and replaced by plain track, but this left a 55mph restriction. In a move to abolish this a curve on a new site was built, enabling the limit to be raised to 85mph. The new curve was brought into use in April 1970.

Towards the end of 1972 improvements took place at the south end of Durham station, and to enable the up and down fast lines to be modified the up platform line was removed and the up fast slewed to take its place: at the same time the platform face was given a gentle curve to iron out the kink at the south end. Moving the up fast allowed the down fast to be slewed to take its place, easing the run off the viaduct for trains not stopping at Durham.

In 1974 further alterations were carried out at Relly Mill and the curve realigned in 1969 was again altered. This time the embankment formerly carrying the Bishop Auckland branch was removed completely and the resulting spoil used to fill in the Bridge House Junction to Baxter Wood Junction spur which passed below it, giving a new formation joining the old at the spot where Bridge House box stood.

On 4 May 1970 the Eastern Region introduced a cheap fare service between Newcastle and Finsbury Park, with a single fare of 35s 0d (£1.75) compared with the normal second class fare of 86s 0d (£4.30) and the coach fare of 38s 0d (£1.90). According to the publicity material issued by the Region the journey was to take 'a little under six hours' whereas the fastest Inter-City time was 3hr 35min. Advance booking was necessary and there were no half fares for children. The service ran under the name 'The Highwayman' but, like its predecessor, the train's movements were hidden behind a cloak of secrecy and it did not appear in the timetable!

More accelerations came into effect on 7 May 1973 and the 07.45 from Kings Cross, now with stops at Stevenage, York and Darlington, was into Newcastle in 213min for the 268miles, beating the 'Flying Scotsman', non-stop over the same distance, by four minutes. However, the fastest down service was provided by the 18.00 from Kings Cross, which with stops at Darlington and Durham, was into Newcastle in 210min. The corresponding up working, the 07.25 from Newcastle, was also allowed 210min, as was the 17.00 from Newcastle. The 'Flying Scotsman' timing was cut

Shed	Shunting Locomotives	Main Line Locomotives	Total	Steam 1950
Leeds (Neville Hill)	5	–	5	76
York	19	38	57	106
Darlington	16	–	16	112
Gateshead	47	135	182	89
Edinburgh (Haymarket)	6	122	128	81
			388	464

by 12min in the up direction and by 13 in the down, making it 5½hr in both directions, including a stop at Newcastle.

These accelerations were largely the result of the improvements at Peterborough where, for far too long, trains had suffered a severe speed restriction through the station. The North Eastern, faced with a similar problem at Darlington, put the main lines outside the station in 1887 when the present Bank Top station was built!

The new timings required some very high-speed running, particularly between Northallerton and York, but all records over this stretch were broken in June 1973 when the prototype High Speed Train, on trial and training runs, achieved first 131mph, then 141mph (on 11 June) followed by 143mph the next day. During these tests the train ran at over 130mph for 22miles, and at 140mph for 3miles!

British Rail subsequently announced that the train would go into normal service from 13 August 1973 on the 08.45 Leeds to Edinburgh and return, but this promise was not fulfilled. On a demonstration run from Kings Cross to Darlington and back on 2 August 1973, carrying a number of invited passengers, an impressive performance was given over the old North Eastern racing stretch from Darlington to York. The 44.1 miles were covered in 27min. 37sec. start to stop, with a maximum speed of 137mph. Northallerton to Thirsk, pass to pass, took only 3min. 31sec. – an average speed of 133.5mph.

But what will happen at this speed if there is a broken rail, or even a broken fishplate? The derailment of the up 'North Briton' near Amble Junction in July 1967 has already been mentioned, and a similar accident took place near Chathill on 28 May 1972, when the 11.00 Edinburgh to Kings Cross express was derailed due to a broken fishplate. The train was travelling at about 82mph, hauled by a 'Deltic' locomotive, when it was derailed, but fortunately it remained almost in line, and although the coaches were damaged below the sole-bars there was no damage above, except for one broken pane of a double-glazed window unit, and no-one was hurt.

'Deltic' No. 9009 *Alycidon* passes Sunderland with an Edinburgh-Kings Cross train diverted because of a derailment near Ferryhill on 15 October 1972./*Ian S. Carr*

Above: 'Deltic' No. 55.006 *The Fife & Forfar Yeomanry* at Darlington with the up 'Flying Scotsman' on 1 January 1975. This train does not normally stop at Darlington but a modified service was operated on New Year's Day./*Ian S. Carr*

Below: Class 47 diesel No. D1504 on a down express at Newton Hall on 30 March 1970. The new alignment for higher speeds was brought into use three weeks later./*Ian S. Carr*

Above: Class 47 No. 1633 passing Monkwearmouth station with an excursion on 7 April 1973. The station buildings are now used as a museum./*Ian S. Carr*

Below: 'Deltic' No. 9018 *Ballymoss* standing at Platform 9 at Newcastle Central with the up 'Tees-Tyne Pullman', and the High Speed Train in Platform 10 en route Leeds to South Gosforth, on 5 July 1973./*Ian S. Carr*

Diesel No. 47.430 on the new alignment south of Relly Mill on 22 September 1974. The up main line is still on the old alignment – to the extreme left./*Ian S. Carr*

Appendix 1

TIMINGS OF THE FLYING SCOTSMAN (10.00am EX KINGS CROSS) 1923–1975

Station		1923	Non-Stop 1928	Non-Stop 1932	Non-Stop 1939	1940	1945	1960**		1975
Shaftholme Junction	(pass)	1.09	1.02	12.55	12.36	1.40	1.27	12.12	12.50	12.06
Selby	(pass)	1.25	1.19	1.11	12.51½	1.56	1.43	12.25	1.03	12.16
York	(arr)	1.45	—	—	—	2.15	2.02	—	—	—
	(pass)	—	1.38	1.29	1.10	—	—	12.40	1.18½	12.29
	(dep.)	1.53	—	—	—	2.21	2.15	—	—	—
Northallerton	(pass)	2.29	2.15	2.02	1.41½	2.56	2.50	1.08	1.46½	12.52
Darlington	(pass)	2.44	2.31	2.16	1.55½	3.13	3.06	1.20	2.02½	1.05
Durham	(pass)	3.12	3.02	2.42	2.21½	3.18	3.35	1.42	2.24½	1.22
Newcastle	(arr)	3.32	—	—	—	4.08	3.55	—	2.45	1.37
	(pass)	—	3.23	3.00	2.39	—	—	1.59	—	—
	(dep.)	3.39	—	—	—	4.14	4.05	—	2.51	1.39
Alnmouth	(pass)	4.22	4.11	3.45	3.21	5.01	4.52	2.36	3.29½	2.11
Berwick	(arr)	4.59	—	—	—	5.38	5.29	—	—	—
	(pass)	—	4.50	4.20	3.56	—	—	3.06	4.03½	2.35
	(dep.)	5.04	—	—	—	5.41	5.34	—	—	—
Edinburgh	(arr.)	6.15	6.08*	5.30	5.00	6.54	6.55	4.05	5.02	3.30
Time in minutes		306	306	275	264	314	328	233	252	204
Stops		3	—	—	—	4	3	—	1	1
Time allowed for stops		20	—	—	—	20	28	—	6	2

* WTT time: public time 6.15.

** At this period the non-stop working was being performed by the 9.30am from Kings Cross (The 'Elizabethan') passing Shaftholme Junction 12.12pm. The 10.0am from Kings Cross (The 'Flying Scotsman') passed Shaftholme Junction at 12.50pm and stopped only at Newcastle.

Appendix 2

Haymarket 3,300hp Locomotive Roster: Summer 1962

	arr		dep	
Monday				
Edinburgh	–		10.00am	
Kings Cross	4.0pm	F	7.30pm	
Tuesday				
Edinburgh	3.00am	M	1.30pm	
Kings Cross	8.23pm	F	10.45pm	
Wednesday				
Leeds	3.22am		7.30am	
Kings Cross	10.30am	F & I	2.00pm	
Edinburgh	9.00pm	F	11.05pm	
Thursday				
Kings Cross	6.48am	F & I	9.40am	
Leeds	2.00pm		5.29pm	
Kings Cross	8.42pm	F	10.30pm	
Friday				
Newcastle	3.49am	F & I	9.40am	
Kings Cross	2.28pm	F & I	8.20pm	
Saturday				
Edinburgh	4.33am	M	–	
Stand pilot	9.00am	to 11.30pm		
Sunday				
Edinburgh	–		10.10am	
Kings Cross	5.49pm	F	10.15pm	
Monday				
Edinburgh	5.00am			

F = Fuel   F & I = Fuel and inspection
M = Maintenance

The above table does not include workings between stations and sheds and/or carriage sidings. Men were changed at Newcastle on all Edinburgh-London workings: men were also changed at York and/or Grantham except where Gateshead or Kings Cross men were working through between Newcastle and London. Haymarket crews did not work south of Newcastle, nor Kings Cross and Grantham crews north of Newcastle. Gateshead crews worked to Edinburgh and London. All passenger trains.

Appendix 3

Gateshead 2,500hp Locomotive Roster: Summer 1962

	arr		dep	
Monday				
Newcastle	–		12.50pm	
Bristol	8.20pm	F	11.45pm	Parcels
Tuesday				
Derby	4.15am		8.12am	
Bristol	11.46am		2.15pm	
York	7.45pm	F	9.15pm	Fish
Wednesday				
Birmingham	2.57am		8.05am	
Newcastle	1.00pm	F	3.30pm	
Birmingham	8.20pm		11.38pm	Parcels
Thursday				
York	4.25am		6.55am	
Newcastle	9.08am	F	12.50pm	
Bristol	8.20pm	F	11.45pm	Parcels
Friday				
Derby	4.15am		8.12am	
Bristol	11.46am		2.15pm	
York	7.45pm	F	9.15pm	Fish
Saturday				
Birmingham	2.57am		8.05am	
Newcastle	1.00pm	F	3.50pm	
Birmingham	8.52pm	F	–	
Sunday				
Birmingham	–		7.55am	
Derby	9.06am	F	–	
Monday				
Derby	–		8.12am	
Bristol	11.58am		2.15pm	
York	7.45pm	F	–	

F = Fuel

Does not include workings between stations and sheds and/or carriage sidings. Passenger trains unless otherwise stated.

Appendix 4

York 2,000hp Locomotive Roster: Summer 1962

	arr		dep	
Monday				
York	–		4.40am	Goods
Gateshead	8.55am		–	
Newcastle	–		2.35pm	
York	4.32pm	F	–	
Tuesday				
York	–		2.04am	News
Newcastle	3.56am		9.23am	ECS
York	1.03pm	F & I	6.37pm	
Newcastle	9.15pm		11.50pm	Parcels
Wednesday				
York	2.16am	M	2.10pm	Goods
Newcastle	4.45pm		6.30pm	LE
Sunderland	7.00pm		8.00pm	Parcels
York	10.25pm		–	
Thursday				
York	–		4.35am	
Leeds	5.10am	F & I	9.10am	
Glasgow	3.07pm		4.00pm	
Leeds	10.04pm	F	–	
Friday				
Leeds	–		1.10am	
York	1.45am		3.50am	
Sunderland	7.37am		–	LE
Newcastle	–		11.15am	Parcels
York	3.40pm	F & I	8.10pm	
Newcastle	9.48pm		–	
Saturday				
Newcastle	–		8.30am	
York	10.17am	F	4.31pm	
Newcastle	6.12pm		8.30pm	
York	10.45pm	F & I	–	
Sunday				
York	–		12.45am	Parcels
Kings Cross	10.31am		7.00pm	Parcels
York	1.15am	F	–	

F=Fuel F & I=Fuel and Inspection
M=Maintenance

Does not include workings between stations and sheds and/or Carriage sidings. Passenger trains unless otherwise stated.

Appendix 5

Routes

Main Line
London-Edinburgh via Shaftholme Junction-York-Darlington-Newcastle-Berwick

Secondary Main Lines
London-Harrogate via Shaftholme Junction-Knottingley-Church Fenton-Wetherby
Harrogate-London (Pullman only) via Harrogate-York- Shaftholme Junction
London-Glasgow (Pullmans only) via Leeds (Central)-Harrogate-Northallerton- Newcastle-Edinburgh
Newcastle-Liverpool via Darlington-Northallerton-Harrogate-Arthington-Leeds (New)
Newcastle-Liverpool via Darlington-Northallerton-Harrogate-Wetherby- Leeds (New)
Newcastle-Liverpool via Darlington- York-Leeds (New)
Newcastle-Liverpool via Sunderland- Stockton-Harrogate-Arthington-Leeds (New)
Newcastle-Liverpool via Sunderland-Stockton-Harrogate-Wetherby-Leeds (New)
Newcastle-Bristol via Darlington-York-Sheffield (Midland)
Newcastle-Hull via Darlington-York (reverse)
Scarborough-Glasgow via Malton (double reversal) -Gilling-Pilmoor- Darlington-Newcastle-Edinburgh

Appendix 6

Diversionary Routes

Shaftholme Junction and York via Knottingley-Church Fenton

Shaftholme Junction and York via Selby Canal-Selby West- Gascoigne Wood-Church Fenton

York-Northallerton via Starbeck-Ripon

Northallerton-Ferryhill via Picton-Eaglescliffe-Stockton-Stillington

Eaglescliffe-Northallerton via Dinsdale-Geneva curve-Croft Spa

Darlington-Durham via Bishop Auckland

Ferryhill-Gateshead via Tursdale Junction-Leamside-Penshaw-Pelaw

Durham-Gateshead via Leamside-Penshaw-Pelaw

Low Fell-Newcastle via Dunston-Scotswood

Sunderland-Stockton via Murton-Thorpe Thewles

Newcastle-Forest Hall via Manors-Gosforth-Benton

Newcastle-Morpeth via Backworth-Bedlington (reversal necessary at Morpeth to proceed northwards)

Newcastle-Edinburgh via Carlisle-Hawick

Tweedmouth-Edinburgh via Kelso-Galashiels

Variations did occur in the face of emergencies.

Class C6 (NER Class V) 4-4-2 No.532 – the first Worsdell Atlantic – on an up fitted meat train at Chester Moor Colliery, on 17 August 1926. Note the express passenger headlights on the locomotive./*H. G. W. Household*